MONETARY, FISCAL AND TRADE POLICIES SERIES

SAVINGS IN THE U.S.: EFFECTS, ISSUES AND PROPOSALS

MONETARY, FISCAL AND TRADE POLICIES SERIES

Challenges of the Post-Communist Financial-Currency Policy
Avtandil Silagadse and Micheil Tokmazishvili
2009. ISBN: 978-1-60741-150-5

U.S. Trade with Developing Countries: Policy, Programs and Trends
Kalan R. Geisler (Editor)
2009 ISBN: 978-1-60741-122-2

Measuring the Economy: GDP and NIPAs
Kemal Sahin (Editor)
2009 ISBN: 978-1-60741-199-4

Trade Policy in A Globalizing World
Yuki Watanabe and Haruto Yamashita (Editors)
2009 ISBN: 978-1-60456-830-1

Savings in the U.S.: Effects, Issues and Proposals
Lyman T. Randolph (Editor)
2010. ISBN: 978-1-60741-357-8

MONETARY, FISCAL AND TRADE POLICIES SERIES

SAVINGS IN THE U.S.: EFFECTS, ISSUES AND PROPOSALS

LYMAN T. RANDOLPH
EDITOR

Nova Science Publishers, Inc.
New York

For permission to use material from this book please contact us:
Telephone 631-231-7269; Fax 631-231-8175
Web Site: http://www.novapublishers.com

LIBRARY OF CONGRESS CATALOGING-IN-PUBLICATION DATA

Savings in the U.S. : effects, issues and proposals / editor, Lyman T. Randolph.
p. cm.
Includes bibliographical references and index.
ISBN 978-1-60741-357-8 (softcover : alk. paper)
1. Saving and investment--United States. 2. Finance, Personal--United States. 3. United States--Economic policy--2009- 4. United States--Economic conditions--2009- I. Randolph, Lyman T.
HC110.S3S28 2009
339.4'30973--dc22

2009032918

Published by Nova Science Publishers, Inc. ✝ New York

CONTENTS

PREFACE

Raising the share of income saved is a frequent aim of public policy. That may be particularly apparent in debates about the size of the federal budget deficit, but concerns about the low household saving rate have also prompted policymakers to consider ways to encourage individuals to save more. How much individuals save will directly affect their future economic well-being. This book presents standard economic analysis of the macroeconomic effects of raising savings. An increase in saving means a reduction in spending. In the short run, that is likely to result in slower economic growth than would otherwise have been the case. When the saving rate rises, demand for financial assets rises as well. This book also looks at savings incentives and Social Security, and why the household savings rate is low. From a macroeconomic perspective, what matters is that saving, whether from the household, business or public sector is channeled into investments which increase the capital stock, raise productivity and add to economic growth.This book consists of public documents which have been located, gathered, combined, reformatted, and enhanced with a subject index, selectively edited and bound to provide easy access.

Chapter 1 - One issue that never seems far from the minds of policymakers is Social Security. At the heart of the issue is the large shortfall of projected revenues needed to meet the mounting costs of the system. For the moment, the amount of Social Security tax receipts exceeds the amount of benefits being paid out. The Social Security trustees estimate that, beginning in 2017, the amount of benefits being paid out will exceed tax collections. According to the trustees' best estimate, the trust fund will be exhausted in the year 2040.

Some have argued that because the Social Security trust fund is intended to meet rising future costs of the program, its surplus should not be counted as contributing to official measures of the budget surplus. With regard to current saving, however, it makes no difference whether the surplus is credited to the trust fund or simply seen as financing current federal government outlays (including Social Security benefits). Off-budget surpluses contribute to national saving in exactly the same way as on budget surpluses do. The additional saving they represent adds to the national saving rate and allows current investment spending to be higher than it would otherwise be.

With respect to household saving for retirement, how much is "enough" may be a subjective matter. But, one standard might be whether accumulated wealth is sufficient to avoid a decline in living standards upon retirement. A number of studies have found, however, that Americans may not tend to save enough to avoid such a decline in their living standard.

Social Security may affect saving in several ways. It may reduce household saving as participants pay some of their Social Security contributions by reducing what they otherwise would have set aside. It reduces the risk associated with retirement planning and so may free participants to cut precautionary saving. It may, however, encourage additional saving by making it possible to retire earlier, thus giving participants a longer period of retirement to plan for. To the extent that Social Security involves a transfer of income from workers to retirees, it tends to reduce household saving by shifting resources from potentially high savers to those who save less.

Proposed reforms have different effects on saving. Those that would move toward a more fully funded system would be likely to increase national saving, investment, and the size of the economy in the future. Reforms that would partially "privatize" using individual accounts, might tend to reduce national saving, unless contributions to those accounts were mandatory. Those that invested Social Security funds in private sector assets would be unlikely to have any effect on national saving. This report will be updated as economic events warrant.

Chapter 2 - Raising the share of income saved is a frequent aim of public policy. That may be particularly apparent in debates about the size of the federal budget deficit, but concerns about the low household saving rate have also prompted policymakers to consider ways to encourage individuals to save more. How much individuals save will directly affect their future economic well-being, but from a macroeconomic perspective, the source of saving — be it households, business, or government — makes no difference. This report presents standard economic analysis of the macroeconomic effects of raising saving.

An increase in saving means a reduction in spending. In the short run, that is likely to result in slower economic growth than would otherwise have been the case. When the saving rate rises, demand for financial assets rises as well. The increase in demand for assets puts upward pressure on their prices and that results in a decline in their yields and so interest rates fall. The decline in interest rates sets in motion a chain of events that tends to reduce the extent to which incomes might fall in response to an increase in the saving rate.

Domestically, lower interest rates reduce the cost of financing expenditures on durable goods as well as business fixed investment, and thus increase some private sector demand. Lower interest rates can also have an effect on the balance of trade. A decline in U.S. interest rates, relative to foreign rates, is likely to reduce foreign purchases of U.S. assets. While an increase in saving may initially cause income to fall relative to what it otherwise would have been, in time any decline in income is likely to be offset by rising investment demand and an increase in net exports.

If there is a one-time permanent increase in the rate of investment, each worker will have more capital with which to work, and there will be a one-time rise in the capital-labor ratio, and thus a one-time rise in labor productivity. The one-time increase in labor productivity will *temporarily* raise the growth rate of output.

If financial capital flows easily between countries, then even a small decline in U.S. interest rates would be likely to have a large influence on the demand for dollardenominated assets. In that case, the net outflow of capital from the U.S. economy would minimize the decline in interest rates. The smaller the decline in interest rates is, the smaller any stimulus to domestic spending will be. In that case, more of the short-term contractionary effect of an increase in saving would be offset by rising net exports than by increased domestic investment.

This report will be updated as warranted.

Chapter 3 - Despite mostly favorable economic conditions since the early 1990s, one development — the focus of this report — may be cause for concern. While the economy was growing, household saving fell to next to nothing. At the beginning of the 1990s, households saved, on average, about 8% of their after-tax income. Since then, it has steadily declined, and since 2005, the proportion of income households set aside has been near zero.

One of the most striking aspects of the economic expansion of the 1990s was the dramatic rise in equity prices. Between 1991 and 2001, the Standard and Poor's index of 500 stock prices rose by 217%, and the NASDAQ stock price index increased by 313%. The standard economic model of saving behavior assumes that households are likely to spend more and save less out of current income given an increase in their wealth. Given that, it seems reasonable to suppose that those increases in equity prices had something to do with the decline in the personal saving rate. A number of studies have found that the decline in the personal saving rate during the 1990s was due at least in part to the rise in equity prices.

The stock market peaked in the second half of 2000. Between September 2000 and October 2002, the S&P 500 fell by 46%. Since then, S&P 500 stock prices have recovered, but they remained slightly below the 2000 peak at the end of 2006. Even though the stock market boom ended, the household saving rate continued to decline. The fact that household saving continued to be anemic even after the stock market cooled suggests that there are other factors that need to be considered. One candidate is the boom in the housing market. Since late 1997, the price of housing has risen rapidly. Between late 1997 and late 2006, house prices doubled, on average. Although there are reasons to think that housing price appreciation might not be a good substitute for saving, a number of empirical studies, while not quite a consensus, found evidence to suggest that it might.

When changes in personal wealth are taken into account, the decline in the official saving measure may be less of an issue, although there will always be concerns about the durability of any gains in asset prices. With respect to the household sector's contribution to total national saving, that has clearly fallen. Meanwhile, investment spending has risen relative to gross domestic product (GDP), in spite of the decline in personal saving, due to the increase in capital inflows from abroad. Some of the productivity gains likely to result from that increased investment, however, will benefit foreign rather than domestic investors. If house price appreciation slows for a long time, households may end up with less wealth than they anticipate. That would make the current low saving rate seem more of a problem.

This report will be updated as developments warrant.

Chapter 4 - Saving is the portion of national output that is not consumed and represents resources that can be used to increase, replace, or improve the nation's capital stock. The U.S. net national saving rate reached a post-war peak of 12.4% in 1965 and has then trended downward since to a low of 1.9% in 2006. Many analysts claim that saving is too low. Among the Organization for Economic Cooperation and Development (OECD) countries, the United States has the third lowest saving rate.

Survey evidence suggests that people know why they should save, but many don't save, especially lower-income individuals and families. Several reasons have been offered to explain the declining personal saving rate and the relatively high proportion of individuals and families that do not save. Economic reasons start from the premise that individuals and families are rational and make optimal decisions about consumption and saving throughout the life course. Low saving rates are then explained by economic disincentives induced by government policy or by life cycle changes in the propensity to save. Behavioral reasons start from the premise that individuals and families do not always make optimal decisions regarding consumption and saving.

The government offers tax incentives to individuals and families to save. The empirical evidence on the relationship of tax incentives to the saving rate mostly comes from examinations of traditional individual retirement accounts (IRAs) and 401(k) plans. The reported results are mixed, but generally indicate small effects. Be that as it may, the tax incentives tend to benefit higher-income individuals and families to a much greater extent than lower-income individuals and families. The primary reasons are (1) higher-income individuals are much more likely to save, and (2) higher-income individuals face higher marginal tax rates and benefit more from sheltering income from taxation.

Furthermore, the tax revenue loss for these incentives lower public saving by reducing the budget surplus or increasing the budget deficit. For FY2007, these tax incentives are estimated to cost the U.S. Treasury $133.8 billion in forgone tax revenues — almost 85% of the estimated FY2007 budget deficit. The Bush Administration and the President's Advisory Panel on Federal Tax Reform have advocated expanding tax incentives as the primary policy to encourage personal saving. Research has shown that personal saving has been fairly unresponsive to tax incentives, however, and such incentives may substantially decrease public saving (that is, increase the budget deficit). The long-term net effect on national saving and economic growth is likely negative.

This report contains historical data and will not bc updated.

Chapter 5 - The amount of money saved has important economic consequences. Nationally, the amount of saving determines how much can be invested and ultimately the size of the capital stock. Increasing the size of the capital stock is believed to be one way to raise the productivity of the labor force. Individually, saving is critical to accumulating sufficient wealth to maintain living standards after retirement. This report explains how national saving is measured, presents recent estimates of saving rates in the United States, and, for comparison, provides those of other major industrial countries. This report will be updated periodically.

Chapter 6 - In various budget proposals, the President proposed to substitute for the current system of tax-favored individual retirement accounts (IRAs) two new accounts: lifetime savings accounts (LSAs) and retirement savings accounts (RSAs). Senator Craig Thomas of the Finance Committee and Representative Sam Johnson of the Ways and Means Committee have introduced identical bills (S. 545/H.R. 1163 and S. 546/H.R. 1162) to create LSAs and RSAs. Expanded savings accounts also were a part of the final recommendations of the President's Advisory Panel on Federal Tax Reform.

These proposals differ from the current system of IRAs in several important ways, including the required use of a back-loaded method now used for Roth but not traditional IRAs (in back-loaded accounts contributions are not deductible but withdrawals are not taxable), higher contribution limits in some cases, introduction of LSAs with no penalties for withdrawal, and elimination of income phaseouts.

Shifting to a mandatory back-loaded method, including the ability to roll over current deductible IRAs into the new system, along with some other features, has important consequences for the path of revenue loss. The Treasury projects the plans to either raise revenue or have little revenue effect in the first 10 years. CRS projections of long-run revenue costs (in the steady state beyond 2015) suggest a 10- year loss in the neighborhood of $300 to $500 billion. While it is difficult to estimate the cost precisely, the large limits and lack of strings attached suggest that a very large fraction of interest, dividends, and capital gains could be tax exempt.

Neither theory nor empirical evidence seems to present much of a case for a significant (or even positive) effect on private savings resulting from these provisions — particularly the back-loaded form. The change would tend to redistribute aftertax income on both a relative and absolute basis from lower- to higher-income groups in part because lower- and moderate-income individuals tend to have little or no savings — although benefits to the highest-income individuals would be constrained by the contributions limit.

The provision of tax favored savings accounts with high limits could have some consequences for certain activities and sectors of the economy. It could reduce the fraction of small businesses with pension plans, as owners elect to save in their private accounts rather than through accounts set up in their businesses. The provisions would also make a variety of currently favored investments less attractive, including tax exempt state and local bonds, life insurance products such as deferred annuities, and direct investments in owner-occupied housing. Some of these effects should increase economic efficiency. The change would discourage equity investment in unincorporated businesses and rental housing and favor investment in debt. It would have uncertain effects on the most heavily taxed investment, corporate equity. This report will not be updated.

In: Savings in the U.S.: Effects, Issues …
Editor: Lyman T. Randolph
ISBN: 978-1-60741-357-8

Chapter 1

SOCIAL SECURITY, SAVING, AND THE ECONOMY

Brian W. Cashell

SUMMARY

One issue that never seems far from the minds of policymakers is Social Security. At the heart of the issue is the large shortfall of projected revenues needed to meet the mounting costs of the system. For the moment, the amount of Social Security tax receipts exceeds the amount of benefits being paid out. The Social Security trustees estimate that, beginning in 2017, the amount of benefits being paid out will exceed tax collections. According to the trustees' best estimate, the trust fund will be exhausted in the year 2040.

Some have argued that because the Social Security trust fund is intended to meet rising future costs of the program, its surplus should not be counted as contributing to official measures of the budget surplus. With regard to current saving, however, it makes no difference whether the surplus is credited to the trust fund or simply seen as financing current federal government outlays (including Social Security benefits). Off-budget surpluses contribute to national saving in exactly the same way as onbudget surpluses do. The additional saving they represent adds to the national saving rate and allows current investment spending to be higher than it would otherwise be.

With respect to household saving for retirement, how much is "enough" may be a subjective matter. But, one standard might be whether accumulated wealth is sufficient to avoid a decline in living standards upon retirement. A number of studies have found, however, that Americans may not tend to save enough to avoid such a decline in their living standard.

Social Security may affect saving in several ways. It may reduce household saving as participants pay some of their Social Security contributions by reducing what they otherwise would have set aside. It reduces the risk associated with retirement planning and so may free participants to cut precautionary saving. It may, however, encourage additional saving by making it possible to retire earlier, thus giving participants a longer period of retirement to plan for. To the extent that Social Security involves a transfer of income from workers to retirees, it tends to reduce household saving by shifting resources from potentially high savers to those who save less.

Proposed reforms have different effects on saving. Those that would move toward a more fully funded system would be likely to increase national saving, investment, and the size of the economy in the future. Reforms that would partially "privatize" using individual accounts, might tend to reduce national saving, unless contributions to those accounts were mandatory. Those that invested Social Security funds in private sector assets would be unlikely to have any effect on national saving. This report will be updated as economic events warrant.

INTRODUCTION

One issue of perennial concern to policymakers is Social Security. At the heart of the issue is the large shortfall of projected revenues needed to meet the mounting costs of the system, beginning in about 2017. Taxes on those currently in the workforce are credited to the trust fund and benefits to retirees are debited from the trust fund. The balance of the fund itself consists of Treasury securities.

At the moment, the amount of tax receipts exceeds the amount of benefits being paid out, and so the balance in the trust fund is growing. The current "best estimate" of the Social Security trustees is that beginning in 2017, the amount of benefits being paid out will exceed tax collections. At that time, the trust fund will have a balance of $4.7 trillion credited to it. According to the trustees' best estimate, the trust fund will be exhausted in the year 2040.[1]

Because benefits are projected to exceed receipts in 2017, there is concern among many policymakers that changes need to be made now. If steps are not taken now, it is argued, much more drastic changes will be needed down the road.

The major function of Social Security is to provide a base upon which to secure the income of the retired population. It does so by transferring income from the working population to those who are no longer in the labor force because of retirement or disability. This is also known as an intergenerational compact, by which those currently working support the retired population with the expectation that future workers will, in turn, provide for their retirement benefits. It also serves a social welfare function, by paying relatively more to retirees who were low-income earners, and survivors and dependents.

From a macroeconomic perspective, however, what matters is the effect on national saving. In a general sense, the economy is blind to the sources of saving. What matters is that saving, whether from the household, business, or public sector is channeled into investments which increase the capital stock, raise productivity and add to economic growth.

If individuals set aside substantial amounts during their working lives then the accumulated wealth and their expected Social Security benefits may be sufficient to provide for their retirement years. The more individuals save for their retirement, the higher their standard of living will be when they retire. If individuals are not saving enough to provide for some minimal standard of living in retirement, then increased saving in the public sector is one way of increasing national resources out of which to fund retirement benefits in the future. The larger the economy, the better able the nation will be to ensure a given minimum standard of living to all retirees.[2]

This paper examines the determinants of household saving and how household saving may be affected by Social Security. The potential effects of possible changes in Social Security on household and national saving are also discussed.[3]

SAVING AND THE ECONOMY

By definition, saving is that proportion of income that is not consumed. Rather, it is made available to sustain and increase the stock of productive capital. Combined with labor and technological advances, it is this capital that contributes to the production of all the goods and services that make up national output.

Reducing the share of income that is consumed and increasing the share that is saved, will tend to raise the amount of capital available to the labor force. The more capital available to the workforce, the greater the production of goods and services will be. In other words, by saving more now, people will be able to consume more in the future.

From a macroeconomic perspective, it makes little if any difference where the saving comes from. In terms of the collective resources of the nation, a dollar of saving means a dollar of investment whether it is household, business, or public sector saving.

The measure that matters with respect to the federal government's saving is the unified budget. For some purposes, the budget is divided into two accounts; one is referred to as "on-budget" and the other is "off-budget." The so-called off-budget surplus consists almost entirely of Social Security receipts and outlays.[4]

Some have argued that Social Security should not be counted as contributing to official measures of the budget surplus. Keeping Social Security off budget is a procedural device by which Congress signals that the Social Security program should be insulated from other operations of the budget. "Lockbox" proposals go further in an attempt to deter the current and future Congresses from using Social Security surpluses to justify spending increases for other federal programs or for tax cuts.[5]

With regard to current saving, however, it makes no difference whether those revenues are credited to the trust fund or simply seen as financing current federal government outlays (including Social Security benefits).[6] Without the excess revenues from Social Security taxes, the deficit would be larger, and the federal government's requirements for a share of the national savings pool would be larger as well. Off-budget surpluses contribute to national saving in exactly the same way as on-budget surpluses do. The additional saving they represent adds to the national saving rate and allows current investment spending to be higher than it would otherwise be.

EXPLAINING HOUSEHOLD SAVING

Any examination of Social Security and its effects on households must begin with an explanation of household saving behavior. What do households take into account when deciding whether, and how much, to save?

Life Cycle Saving

Most economists analyze household saving behavior using what is known as the life-cycle model of consumer behavior. The life-cycle model begins with the basic assumption that most individuals are not myopic but rather take their expected lifetimes into account when deciding how much out of current income to save and how much to spend.

The life-cycle model assumes that individuals seek to avoid large fluctuations in their standard of living over the course of their lifetimes. The model further takes as a given that individuals' incomes tend to follow a predictable pattern over the course of their lifetimes. Typically, that would mean relatively low levels of income during the initial years of work, increases in income up to retirement, and then a drop in income during retirement.

If consumption followed the same pattern as income, it would make for substantial changes in living standards over the course of a lifetime. Instead, consumers are presumed to vary the rate at which they save out of income in order to dampen the effect of changes in income on consumption. Thus, the typical pattern would be that individuals save relatively little in the early stages of their working lives. Then, during peak earning years, saving rates tend to be higher in order to accumulate wealth off of which to live during retirement, when saving tends to fall off considerably.[7]

Precautionary Saving

There is a second consideration that may motivate household saving in addition to retirement. While there may be a typical pattern to incomes, on average, over lifetimes, there is also a certain amount of uncertainty associated with an individual's income at a given time in the future. For example, some incomes vary over the course of the business cycle, and from time to time people may also experience episodes of either voluntary or involuntary unemployment. Thus, in addition to serving as a buffer against lifetime income fluctuations, some fraction of saving may also act to insure against the risks of shorter-term fluctuations in income. This kind of saving may also help to insure against whatever risk might be associated with an individual's pension plan. It is generally referred to as precautionary saving.

Although this may not account for all the possible incentives households have to save, it is enough of a framework to make some general observations about household saving behavior. For example, a temporary decline in incomes will not necessarily have an effect on consumer spending, or on an individual's long-term saving rate, since households have already set funds aside for just such a rainy day. But, any change in prospects that are likely to extend over an entire lifetime might well affect saving behavior.

Recent Trends in Household Saving

Social Security was created to help secure the economic condition of the retired population by forcing them to save more now in exchange for expected future benefits. Concern remains, however, that many are still not setting aside enough on their own in order to provide adequately for retirement.[8]

It has often been noted that Americans save less than they used to, and that they save less than most other industrialized nations. Those concerns were part of the motivation for the policies that contributed to the elimination of the federal budget deficit.[9] Personal saving, as measured in the standard economic accounts, has been falling steadily since 1990. **Figure 1** shows personal saving as a percentage of aftertax personal income since 1970. The personal saving rate has fallen steadily from more than 10% in the early 1980s to less than zero in 2006.

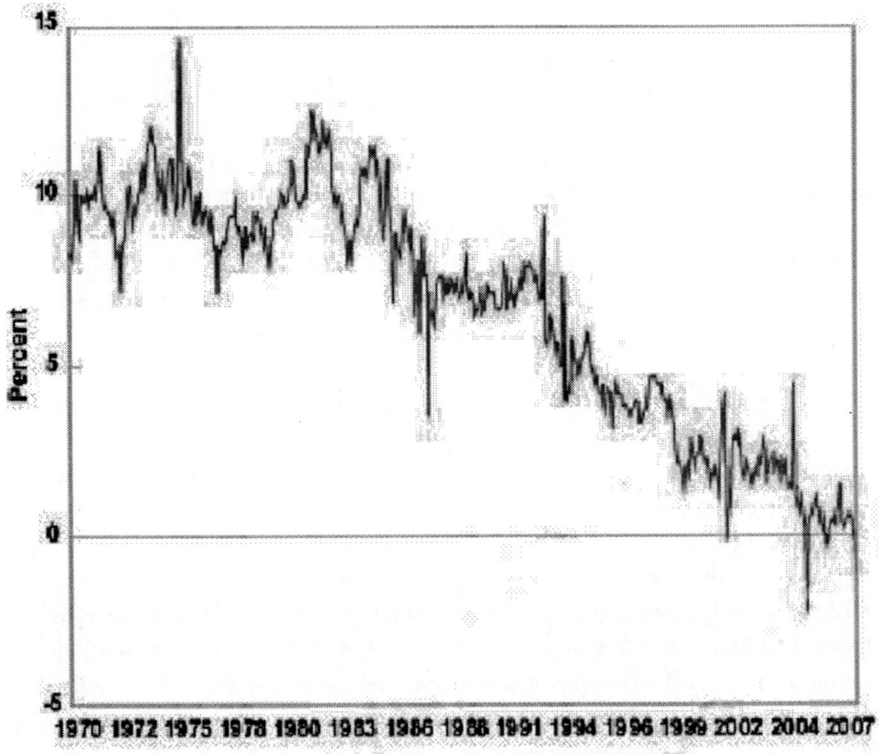

Source: Department of Commerce, Bureau of Economic Analysis.

Figure 1. Personal Saving as a Percentage of Aftertax Personal Income

However, this measure of saving may give an exaggerated picture of the drop in saving. One of the most marked characteristics of the economy during much of the 1990s was the dramatic rise in equity prices. But, capital gains are not included in the measure of saving shown in **Figure 1**. A measure of saving based on changes in household net worth would tell a different story. In fact, much of the decline in measured savings, at least through 1999, may have been due to a large increase in equity prices. Between 1990 and 1999, total household net worth more than doubled, while the ratio of household net worth to aftertax income rose from 472% to 633%.[10] The increase in wealth resulting from the rise in equity prices may have led some to feel they did not need to save as much.[11]

Between 1999 and 2003, however, equity prices fell by about one-third, and during that period, the saving rate continued to decline. Stock prices have since recovered, but that household saving continued to be anemic even after the stock market cooled suggests that there are other factors that need to be considered. One candidate would seem to be the boom in the housing market. Since late 1997, the price of housing has risen rapidly relative to prior years. Between the third quarters of 1997 and 2007, the house price index published by the Office of Federal Housing Enterprise Oversight (OFHEO) doubled.

A number of studies have suggested that housing price appreciation may have had a significant effect on household saving. Belsky and Prakken, for example, found that in the long run, the effects on household saving of house and equity price variations were similar.[12] They also found that house price appreciation had a more immediate effect and that the effect of equity price appreciation took longer to be fully reflected in the saving rate. The authors suggested that may be because historically equity prices have been more volatile than house prices, and so households may be more confident in the durability of house price gains. The authors also indicated that the strong effect of the post-2000 boom in house prices may have been partly due to the simultaneous decline in interest rates, which encouraged homeowners to refinance as well as borrow. They left open the question of whether, in other circumstances, house price appreciation would have the same effect on household saving.[13]

Although there are reasons to think that housing price appreciation might not be a substitute for saving, the empirical studies, not quite amounting to a consensus, found evidence to suggest that it might. If house prices come down in the future, however, households will end up with less wealth than they anticipate. That would make the current low saving rate seem more of a problem.

With respect to household saving, how much is "enough" may be a subjective matter. One standard might be whether accumulated wealth is sufficient to avoid a decline in living standards upon retirement. The life cycle model discussed above assumes that individuals seek to avoid substantial ups and downs in consumption over the course of a lifetime. It might be assumed, then, that the goal of retirement saving is to avoid a significant drop in living standards after retirement.

A number of studies have found, however, that Americans may not save enough to avoid such a decline in their living standard. One, by Hamermesh, of consumption patterns over time found that accumulated wealth, both private and through Social Security, was not sufficient to sustain consumption in early retirement. This study found that, typically, households gradually reduced their consumption spending within several years of having retired.[14]

A more recent study, by Bernheim and Scholz, also found that Americans were not saving enough to prepare for retirement.[15] In particular, they found a distinct difference in saving behavior between those with a college education and the rest of the population. In general, those households with a college education were found to have saved enough to avoid a substantial cutback in consumption on retiring, whereas those with less than a college education had not.[16]

In a separate study of household saving behavior, Bernheim concluded that the typical baby-boom household was saving at about one-third the rate at which they would need to save in order to continue to maintain their current standard of living into retirement.[17]

Engen, Gale, and Uccello make several interesting points regarding the adequacy of household saving for retirement. First, they point out that the ups and downs of the stock market may have little effect on many of those households that are not saving enough, since the ownership of financial assets is heavily concentrated among those households likely to already be saving enough. Second, with regard to what level of saving is considered adequate, it is important to consider the large increase in the consumption of leisure when comparing consumption before and after retirement. Those studies that do not account for the value of leisure time may overestimate the extent of any decline in post-retirement consumption.[18]

Social Security and Household Saving

Social Security was intended to provide a base upon which to secure the income of the retired population. As such, it might have been expected to increase the national rate of saving by adding to what households were already setting aside.

However, there is an important question as to whether or not Social Security is a close substitute for personal saving. If it is, Social Security may lead individuals to save less than they would have in its absence.

Consider the stereotypical saver described by the life cycle model discussed above. How would the introduction of a program which required workers to contribute to a retirement fund for their own eventual benefit affect their saving behavior? Whether and how much individual savings are affected by the introduction of such a program would likely depend on the specific features of the program. Suppose that the contributions yielded the same return as other forms of financial assets households might otherwise buy with their saving. In that case, it might be reasonable to expect that individuals would be indifferent between either saving directly or via the contributions to their retirement fund. The introduction of such a program might simply cause individuals to reduce other saving to offset the amount of their contribution.

Suppose, however, that when the program is introduced, retirement benefits are immediately available to everyone who is qualified. This would be closer to a payas- you-go system. In this case, those who were very near retirement would contribute relatively little to the program while still receiving the full stream of benefits in retirement. Because those who immediately receive benefits would have contributed little to the program there would be a significant transfer of income from those still working to those in retirement.

Of these two groups, workers tend to save more than do those who are retired. The transfer of income from relatively high savers to relatively low savers would tend to bring down the overall household saving rate. In a strictly pay-as-you-go pension system there would be no offsetting saving on the part of the public sector; all of the contributions would be distributed. Thus, the introduction of a pure pay-as-you go Social Security system would tend to reduce the national saving rate.

Another way in which Social Security might influence saving was suggested by economist Martin Feldstein. Feldstein argued that Social Security, or any pension for that matter, might lead people to retire sooner than they otherwise would have. For one thing, once covered workers become eligible for an annuity, their pay effectively drops by the amount of the annuity, since they are only working for the difference between their earnings and what their annuity would be.

In an effort to measure the effect of Social Security on saving, Feldstein examined the effect of Social Security wealth on personal saving using data from 1930 to 1992. Social Security wealth was defined as the discounted present value of promised Social Security benefits. Feldstein found that, for each dollar increase in Social Security wealth, personal savings fell by two or three cents.[19] Other studies on the effect of changes in wealth on household saving have found that for each dollar increase in household wealth, saving out of current income falls by somewhere between 1 cent and 7 cents.[20]

If Social Security encourages workers to retire early, then there is a longer period of retirement to save for. But, workers anticipating an earlier retirement might tend to save more on their own. That aspect of Social Security might then tend to raise the personal saving rate. There are two potentially offsetting effects — Social Security substituting for personal saving, and encouraging longer retirement. The first effect tends to reduce personal saving, the second tends to raise it.

Social Security may also affect the precautionary motive for saving. Social Security, as it now stands, is a defined benefit program. In other words, retirement benefits, although they are based on career earnings, are fixed in real terms upon retirement. After that, they do not vary and continue as long as the beneficiary survives. In contrast, were individuals to provide entirely for their own retirement, there would be several sources of risk. For example, there would be uncertainty regarding how long a period of retirement would have to provided for, and there would be some risk associated with those investments which make up individuals' nest eggs.

Thus, Social Security may affect saving in several ways. It may reduce household saving as participants pay some of their Social Security contributions by reducing what they otherwise would have set aside in other investments. It reduces the risk associated with retirement planning and so may free participants to cut precautionary saving. It may also encourage additional saving by making it possible to retire earlier thus providing participants a longer period of retirement to plan for. To the extent that Social Security involves a transfer of income from workers to retirees, it tends to reduce total saving by shifting resources from high savers to relatively low savers.

SAVING AND SOCIAL SECURITY REFORM

As it now stands, Social Security is partially funded. In 2017, benefit payments are projected to exceed tax receipts and, if that happens, will have to be funded out of general revenues. Because of that, some policymakers urged that changes need to be made. The argument is that whatever costs there are to assuring future benefit payments and boosting the confidence of participants in the program will be more easily borne if they are spread out over a long period of time rather than put off until some inevitable day of reckoning.[21]

In the long run, from a national perspective, what matters is how much people save now. Whether it is household saving, business saving, or a federal budget surplus, increased saving means increased investment, a larger capital stock, and higher future living standards. The more that is saved now, the larger the economy will be in the future. If Social Security is changed, those changes could affect saving in one way or another. Using the basic model of life-cycle and precautionary saving explained above it is possible to make a few relevant observations about the potential effects of various kinds of Social Security reform proposals on saving.[22]

There are two broad kinds of reform possibilities that have been most discussed. One is a shift towards a fully-funded plan. The second is a switch from the *defined benefits* that currently characterize Social Security to one that is at least partly a *defined contribution* plan with variable benefits. This second kind of proposal includes some of the suggestions that would privatize some or all of the Social Security program. Another proposal that has been advanced would have some of the trust fund invested in private securities such as corporate stock.

Fully Funded vs. Pay as You Go

If Social Security were fully funded, that would mean that each generation contributed enough to fully provide for their benefits on retirement, and there would be no intergenerational transfers. A pure pay-as-you-go system, on the other hand, would have no trust fund at all, and all Social Security retirement benefits would be paid for by the current contributions of the working population. In this case there would be a continuing transfer of income between generations. Because Social Security is only partially funded, at some point in the future all benefits will be transfers from the working population to retirees if no changes are made.

Switching to a more fully funded program would necessarily involve some combination of increased contributions and reduced benefits. However, any increase in taxes, or cut in benefits, might be partially offset by a reduction in other forms of household saving. A reduction in benefits could also lead households to save less as they seek to maintain a constant level of consumption given a cut in income. For those still working, a cut in prospective benefits might encourage additional saving.

A shift towards a fully funded system would also tend to reduce the intergenerational redistribution of income. A pure pay-as-you-go system takes income from workers, who tend to be savers, and gives it to retirees who tend to save relatively little. In a fully funded system, workers would finance their own retirement benefits. Shifting from a pay-as-you-go system to a fully funded one might reduce the overall bias against saving which is due to the shift of income from savers to dissavers.

Shifting Social Security closer to a fully funded program might also increase confidence on the part of participants that future benefits would be paid. This might serve to diminish the precautionary incentive to save and tend to reduce household saving.

A shift toward a more fully funded system might lead to a reduction in measured household saving, but it is unlikely that the reduction in household saving would offset the increase in public sector saving. The net result is that such a shift would be likely to raise the national saving rate.

Defined Benefit vs. Defined Contribution

Other proposals for Social Security reform involve at least a partial shift from a *defined benefit* plan to a *defined contribution* plan. A defined benefit plan is one where the benefits are set in advance, and while participants must contribute, their benefits do not depend on the performance of those assets in which they are invested. Participants in a defined contribution retirement plan contribute a set amount periodically into an account, and their ultimate retirement benefits depend on the return on the investments held in those accounts.

Depending on the existing level of confidence in future benefits, a shift toward a defined contribution plan might involve an increase in the perceived, or actual, risk faced by participants. To some extent, future benefits would depend on the performance of those assets in which contributions were invested. An increase in risk might lead households to save more for precautionary reasons. A switch toward a defined contribution plan might not, however, involve a great increase in perceived risk given the apparent skepticism among those working now as to whether or not they will get their full Social Security benefits on retiring. If the assets in which the defined contributions are invested yield a higher return, participants might have an incentive to reduce other forms of saving.

Switching to a defined contribution plan, or partially privatizing Social Security, would reduce the federal government surplus because money that had been collected as taxes would be invested directly by individuals. The measured household saving rate would go up as households themselves invested those funds which previously had been paid into the Social Security trust fund. If these new contributions were mandatory, there would be no net effect on national saving as the increase in household saving would offset the decrease in federal government saving.

If the defined contributions were not mandatory, however, it is possible that the household saving would not rise enough to offset the decline in the federal government saving rate. Many would be likely to spend at least a portion of the reduction in taxes and some, who might not ever plan to retire might spend all of it. Unless the contributions were made mandatory, the net effect of a switch in the direction of a defined contribution plan could reduce the national saving rate.

There could also be some indirect effects on saving. For example, there might be some increase in the risk associated with retirement savings with a switch to a defined contribution plan which could encourage additional precautionary saving.

Investing the Trust Fund in Private Securities

Another reform proposal that has been advanced is that some of the Social Security trust fund, which currently consists exclusively of Treasury securities, be invested in private securities. Such a change would have no effect on national saving.[23]

If the trust fund were to invest in private securities, corporate stock for example, it would have to either sell some of the Treasury securities it now holds or it would buy stocks out of current tax receipts, and the Treasury would have to find another market for any securities it would otherwise issue to the trust fund. In any case, the supply of Treasury securities would increase, their prices would tend to go down, and their yields would tend to go up. At the same time the demand for corporate stock would increase, and the yield on those stocks would tend to fall. Ultimately the public sector would own some private assets, and the private sector would hold a larger proportion of public sector debt. The only change would be in how the public and private sectors invested their money. There is no evidence indicating that households would increase, or reduce, their saving simply as a result of a shift in relative rates of return on selected financial assets.

If trust fund assets were invested in private sector securities, which yielded a higher rate of return, the trust fund might be made better off. But the improvement in the trust fund would come at the expense of the rest of the federal government budget and those private investors that would otherwise have purchased those assets. The borrowing costs of the federal government would rise because of the increased supply of government securities. The income from capital of other private investors would fall because the increase in demand for private sector securities would be likely to reduce their rate of return.[24]

If individual accounts were created out of trust fund assets and those accounts were invested in private securities the situation would be similar. If Social Security funds were held in personal accounts and invested in private securities, their yield would likely be higher than if they were invested in government securities. But, someone would have to buy the assets that would otherwise have been purchased by the trust fund. And those who did would experience a drop in income from capital.

None of this is to say that investing the trust fund in private securities is undesirable, or would have no effect. Rather, it is to say that such a change would be unlikely to affect the national saving rate.

Social Security will never function exactly like a collective retirement plan where each individual sets aside a given amount in order to provide for his own retirement. Even with a fully funded plan, there will be income transfers among participants. For example, those who live longer than average will gain at the expense of those who die prematurely. As long as the plan is less than fully funded, there will be an ongoing transfer from the working population to those who are already retired.

In the case of individuals, how much they set aside during their working years will determine how well they live in retirement. Similarly, for the nation as a whole, how much people save now will play a role in the size of the economy in the future. The collective saving of households, business, and the public sector will determine how much is invested. The more people invest, the larger a stock of capital people will have and the more productive the labor force will be. A more productive labor force means higher standards of living in the future.

By saving more now, the economy in the future will be larger than it otherwise would be. The larger the economy is and the higher incomes are will make it easier to afford paying retirement benefits no matter how they are financed

End Notes

[1] The trustees publish three estimates using different assumptions about costs. They call the intermediate projection their "best estimate." This refers to both Old-Age and Survivors Insurance (OASI) and Disability Insurance (DI), which collectively are referred to as OASDI. See the 2007 OASDI trustee's report, at [http://www.ssa.gov/OACT/TR/TR07/].

[2] A larger economy will make it relatively easier to provide retirement benefits. In dealing with the long-range Social Security funding problem, for example, a larger economy would ease any actions needed to fully fund benefit obligations. Increasing federal government saving now reduces outstanding federal debt and reduces outlays now devoted to financing the existing public sector debt.

[3] For a more comprehensive discussion of Social Security reform proposals, see CRS Report RL31498, *Social Security Reform: Economic Issues*, by Jane Gravelle and Marc Labonte.

[4] The Postal Service is also included in the off-budget account.

[5] Some proponents of accounting devices that isolate Social Security from the rest of the budget claim that this would result in greater government saving. This assumes that spending and tax policy decisions depend on what happens to the trust fund.

[6] Neither would it matter with respect to Social Security deficits, currently projected to begin in 2017.

[7] People with higher incomes tend to save more than those with lower incomes; not necessarily just because their incomes are higher, but also because they are more likely to be in their peak earning years.

[8] Social Security is not the only source of retirement income. In fact, in the national income and product accounts published by the Department of Commerce, contributions to Social Security are not counted as part of household saving.

[9] Such as the omnibus Budget Reconciliation Act of 1993, which included both tax increases and spending cuts. There has also been a reduction in defense spending relative to GDP. See Alberto Alesina, "The Political Economy of the Budget Surplus in the United States," *Journal of Economic Perspectives*, vol.14, no. 3, summer 2000, pp. 3-19.

[10] Figures are from the Board of Governors of the Federal Reserve System.

[11] See CRS Report RL33168, *Why is the Household Saving Rate So Low?* by Brian W. Cashell.

[12] Eric Belsky and Joel Prakken, "Housing's Impact on Wealth Accumulation, Wealth Distribution and Consumer Spending," National Association of Realtors National Center for Real Estate Research, 2004, 26 pp.

[13] Whether or not house price appreciation might substitute for other forms of saving may depend on if there is a strong bequest motive for saving. Those who save in order to leave a bequest to their children may desire to leave a larger bequest if their children are expected to face higher house prices.

[14] Daniel S. Hamermesh, Consumption During Retirement: The Missing Link in the Life Cycle, *The Review of Economics and Statistics*, vol. LXVI, no. 1, February 1984, pp. 1-7.

[15] B. Douglas Bernheim and John Karl Scholz, "Do Americans Save Too Little?," Federal Reserve Bank of Philadelphia *Business Review*, September-October 1993, pp. 3-20.

[16] Income and education tend to be correlated, as are saving and income. Nonetheless, Bernheim and Scholz suggest that one reason some save less than others is that they may not be fully aware of the importance of saving, and that education might be effective in encouraging them to save more.

[17] American Council for Capital Formation, Center for Policy Research, *Special Report*, "Do Households Appreciate Their Financial Vulnerabilities? An Analysis of Actions, Perceptions, and Public Policy," August 1994.

[18] Eric M. Engen, William G. Gale, and Cori Uccello, *Are Households Saving Adequately for Retirement? A Progress Report on Three Projects*, paper presented at the third annual conference of the Retirement Research Consortium, May 2001, p. 19.

[19] Martin Feldstein, "Social Security and Saving: New Time Series Evidence," *National Tax Journal*, June 1996, vol. 49, no. 2, pp. 151-164.

[20] CRS Report RL30518, *The Stock Market and the Economic Outlook*, by Brian W. Cashell. (Out of print; for copies, contact author, 202-707-7816.)

[21] In principle, the Social Security trust fund represents the obligation of the federal government to pay future benefits. In practice, in an economic sense, it is current Social Security receipts and outlays that matter.

[22] See Eric M. Engen and William G. Gale, "Effects of Social Security Reform on Private and National Saving," in *Social Security Reform: Links to Saving, Investment, and Growth*, Federal Reserve Bank of Boston, Conference Series No. 41. June, 1997, pp. 103-142.

[23] Under current rules, if the trust fund purchased private sector securities, those expenditures would be counted as outlays in the unified budget. The increase in measured outlays would reduce the unified budget surplus. But, federal government saving would not change. The Congressional Budget Office is considering changing they way they count purchases of private securities in the budget to eliminate this inconsistency. Whether budget policy depends in any way on particular accounting practices is an issue beyond the scope of this paper. For a discussion, see Congressional Budget Office, Cost Estimate H.R. 4844, Railroad Retirement and Survivors' Improvement Act of 2000.

[24] That is, unless the yields on government bonds had to rise so much, and the yields on the private securities purchased by the trust fund had to fall so much to allow the markets to clear that the shift resulted in no change in capital income to either the private sector or the trust fund.

In: Savings in the U.S.: Effects, Issues ...
Editor: Lyman T. Randolph ISBN: 978-1-60741-357-8

Chapter 2

The Economic Effects of Raising National Saving

Brian W. Cashell

Summary

Raising the share of income saved is a frequent aim of public policy. That may be particularly apparent in debates about the size of the federal budget deficit, but concerns about the low household saving rate have also prompted policymakers to consider ways to encourage individuals to save more. How much individuals save will directly affect their future economic well-being, but from a macroeconomic perspective, the source of saving — be it households, business, or government — makes no difference. This report presents standard economic analysis of the macroeconomic effects of raising saving.

An increase in saving means a reduction in spending. In the short run, that is likely to result in slower economic growth than would otherwise have been the case. When the saving rate rises, demand for financial assets rises as well. The increase in demand for assets puts upward pressure on their prices and that results in a decline in their yields and so interest rates fall. The decline in interest rates sets in motion a chain of events that tends to reduce the extent to which incomes might fall in response to an increase in the saving rate.

Domestically, lower interest rates reduce the cost of financing expenditures on durable goods as well as business fixed investment, and thus increase some private sector demand. Lower interest rates can also have an effect on the balance of trade. A decline in U.S. interest rates, relative to foreign rates, is likely to reduce foreign purchases of U.S. assets. While an increase in saving may initially cause income to fall relative to what it otherwise would have been, in time any decline in income is likely to be offset by rising investment demand and an increase in net exports.

If there is a one-time permanent increase in the rate of investment, each worker will have more capital with which to work, and there will be a one-time rise in the capital-labor ratio, and thus a one-time rise in labor productivity. The one-time increase in labor productivity will *temporarily* raise the growth rate of output.

If financial capital flows easily between countries, then even a small decline in U.S. interest rates would be likely to have a large influence on the demand for dollardenominated assets. In that case, the net outflow of capital from the U.S. economy would minimize the decline in interest rates. The smaller the decline in interest rates is, the smaller any stimulus to domestic spending will be. In that case, more of the short-term contractionary effect of an increase in saving would be offset by rising net exports than by increased domestic investment.

This report will be updated as warranted.

INTRODUCTION

Just as individuals must decide how much of their income to save and how much to spend, firms must decide how much of their profits to pay out as dividends and how much to reinvest, and government must decide how much to tax and how much to spend. Collectively, these choices determine our national rate of saving. From a macroeconomic perspective, however, the source of saving — be it households, business, or government — makes no difference.

Raising the share of income saved is a frequent aim of public policy. That may be particularly apparent in debates about the size of the federal budget deficit, but concerns about the low household saving rate have also prompted policymakers to consider ways to encourage individuals to save more.

One way to interpret the saving rate is as an expression of the collective importance of present versus future consumption. In other words, those who tend to live for the present and discount the future are likely to save at a lower rate than those for whom thrift is a virtue and who hope to maintain their standard of living into retirement.

Variations in the national saving rate can have substantial effects on the economy, and those effects are quite different depending on the time frame under consideration. While saving more may have its benefits, the immediate effect is a decline in consumption. This report examines what economics has to say about both the short- and long-run effects of an increase in the national saving rate on economic growth.

Components of National Saving

Put most simply, the saving rate refers to the share of total income that is not consumed. Saving, and consuming less than all of today's income, makes it possible to consume more tomorrow than would otherwise be possible.

There are multiple sources of saving. Households, or individuals, save in order to maintain living standards into retirement and to insulate themselves from temporary variations in income due to changing economic conditions. Businesses save when they do not pay out all of their profits in the form of dividends. As long as businesses are presented with profitable investment opportunities they will likely retain some earnings in order to take advantage of them. The public sector can also be a source of domestic saving. When tax revenues exceed public outlays, government is a net contributor of saving to the economy. When revenues are insufficient to cover outlays the public sector dis-saves. In other words, saving that might have gone for other uses goes to pay for current government spending. Together, households, businesses, and government account for total national saving.[1]

An Increase in Saving: Short-Run Effects

Suppose policymakers decide that, for whatever reason, the nation is not saving enough and enact legislation to raise the national saving rate. That might take the form of a reduction in the federal budget deficit, or a policy designed to encourage individuals to save more of their income.[2] What would be the immediate consequences for economic growth?

Personal saving equals income less consumption. An increase in saving thus requires a reduction in consumption spending. If the level of consumption spending is what determines living standards then current living standards will fall. If individuals consume less then the effect is direct. If government saves more (or dissaves less) it will be due either to a cut in outlays or an increase in taxes. That means either individuals have less income out of which to consume or government itself is spending less.

In either case, an increase in saving means a reduction in spending. In the short run, that is likely to result in slower economic growth than would otherwise have been the case. To see that, remember that gross domestic product (GDP) is the sum of personal consumption spending, investment spending, government spending and net exports (exports minus imports). Other things being equal, in this elementary accounting framework, a reduction in either government or consumer spending will reduce GDP by an equal amount. Further, any reduction in spending would be reflected in incomes lower than they otherwise would be, at least in the short term.

Each dollar of spending represents income for those who supply the goods and services being bought. A dollar less in spending means a dollar less of income for those producers. Part of each dollar less in income would come out of spending, and part would come out of saving. Suppose that each initial dollar decline in spending resulted in an additional decline in spending of 75 cents. Total income would now have fallen by $1.75. That additional 75 cent decline in spending would result in a 75 cent decline in income. That 75 cent decline in income would then result in an further decline in spending of 56 cents (.75 x .75), and so it would continue in a kind of chain reaction. Total income would now have fallen by $2.31. Each successive decline in income resulting from this chain of events would get smaller and smaller.

If the sequence continued indefinitely, other things being equal, the total decline in income for each dollar increase in saving (decline in spending) would be:

$$1 + .75 + (.75 \times .75) + (.75 \times .75 \times .75) + \ldots$$

Which reduces to:

$$\frac{1}{(1 - 0.75)}$$

Continuing with the simplified example and assuming that each dollar cut in income resulted in a 75 cent cut in spending, an increase of $1 of saving would ultimately yield a reduction in income and output of $4. In the jargon of economics, this is often referred to as the multiplier effect.[3]

If that were the end of the story, it would seem to make raising the saving rate a much less attractive policy goal given the large effects on income and production. But there are a number of other factors to consider. The full effect on incomes of an increase in the saving rate is not likely to be instantaneous. If there is a multiplier effect, it is likely to take time to develop rather than occur all at once. Other factors will come into play and tend ultimately to offset any decline in incomes associated with an increase in the saving rate.

When the saving rate rises, demand for financial assets can be expected to rise as well.[4] The increase in demand for assets puts upward pressure on their prices and that results in a decline in their yields and so interest rates fall. The decline in interest rates sets in motion a chain of events that tends to reduce the extent to which incomes might fall in response to an increase in the saving rate.

Domestically, lower interest rates reduce the cost of financing expenditures on durable goods as well as business fixed investment, and thus increase some private sector demands. In the case of business investment, lower financing costs mean an increase in the number of investment opportunities that are profitable. In the case of consumer spending, lower interest rates may stimulate demand for those goods that are typically debt financed, housing and automobiles being the most important examples.

Lower interest rates can also have an effect on the balance of trade. A decline in U.S. interest rates, relative to foreign rates, is likely to reduce foreign purchases of U.S. assets. If yields on foreign assets rise relative to those on dollar-denominated assets both foreign and domestic investors are likely to increase the share of foreign assets they hold. In order to do that, Americans must first buy the currency in which those assets are denominated and sell dollars.

If foreign demand for dollar-denominated assets falls, the demand for dollars in exchange markets will also fall. Both the increased supply of dollars and the increased demand for other currencies will tend to drive down the value of the dollar in foreign exchange markets. When the dollar falls in value, it makes imported goods more expensive for American consumers and makes American-made goods less expensive for foreign consumers. The result is thus likely to be a decline in imports and an increase in exports.

While an increase in saving may initially cause income to fall relative to what it otherwise would have been, in time any decline in income is likely to be offset by rising investment demand and an increase in net exports. Whether investment spending or net exports is more affected depends in part on how easy it is for financial capital to cross national borders.

If financial capital flows easily between countries, then even a small decline in U.S. interest rates would be likely to have a large influence on the demand for dollardenominated assets. In that case, the net outflow of capital from the U.S. economy would minimize the decline in interest rates. The smaller the decline in interest rates is, the smaller any stimulus to domestic spending will be. In that case, more of the short-term contractionary effect of an increase in saving would be offset by rising net exports than by increased domestic investment.

Feldstein and Horioka published, in 1980, a widely cited paper suggesting that capital did not easily cross international borders, and their evidence was that for a large number of developed countries, variations in domestic saving and investment were highly correlated. That is, when saving rose domestic investment tended to rise as well.[5]

However, there is also evidence that since that paper was published capital mobility has increased substantially.[6] In part because of floating exchange rates and the reduction in capital controls, the volume of international capital flows, at least among developed countries, has increased substantially. If capital is more free to cross borders, a rise in domestic saving is more likely to affect the balance of trade and raise net exports than it is the level of domestic investment.

A key short-run issue is how long it takes for any decline in income due to an increase in the saving rate to be offset by rising investment and net exports. It takes time for the full effects of the increase in saving to be felt on incomes, and it takes time for any consequent decline in interest rates to boost investment and net exports.

No two macroeconomic models agree completely on either the magnitude of the effect or its duration. A 1988 comparison of various models suggested that the ultimate size of the multiplier was somewhere between one and two, meaning that the peak decline in total income would be from \$1 to \$2 for each \$1 increase in saving. Further, that peak effect was estimated to occur about a year or two after the increase in saving.[7] More recently, it has been suggested that the multiplier may be closer to one, if not smaller.[8]

At some point, any effects of higher saving on the level of income are likely to dissipate. Once incomes make up any short-run losses, the only likely durable economic change will be in the composition of income. To the extent that the composition of income changes that may have important long-run consequences.

The past 15 years have seen some substantial swings in the rate of national saving, largely as a result of the federal government budget going from substantial deficits to large surpluses, and then back into deficit. In addition, beginning in the mid-1980s, there was a pronounced decline in the household saving rate.

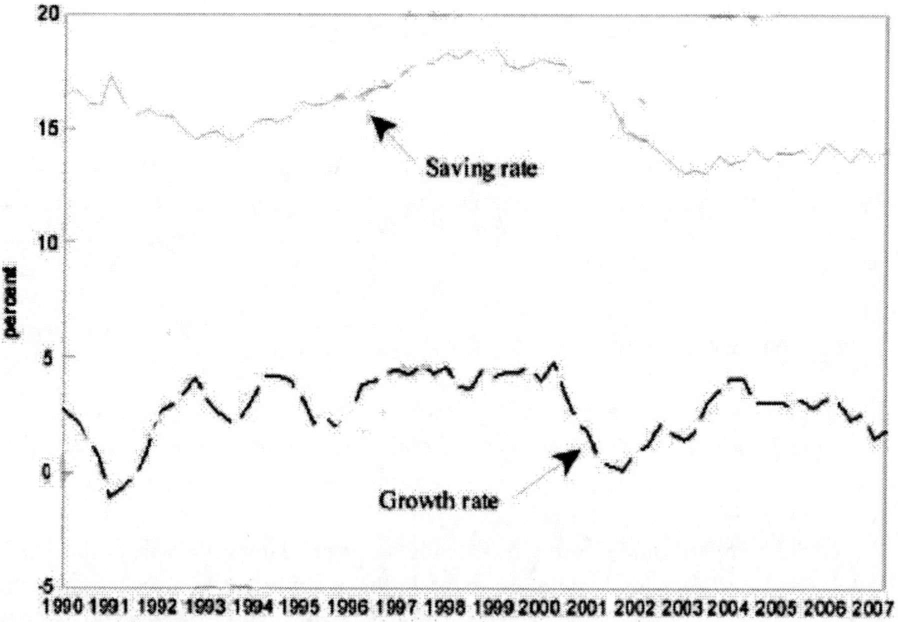

Source: Department of Commerce, Bureau of Economic Analysis.

Figure 1. Saving and Economic Growth Rates

Figure 1 compares the gross national saving rate with the rate of growth of real gross domestic product (GDP) between 1990 and 2007. While theory suggests that a rising saving rate might tend to slow economic growth, it would be hard to find evidence of that in these data.

It may simply be that the models overstate the potential effects of changes in saving on the economy. Another reason for the apparent absence of a connection in recent experience is that the theoretical connection assumes that "other things" stay the same — but in fact that is rarely the case. One thing in particular that might not stay the same is monetary policy.

Because of the ease with which capital flows across international boundaries, monetary policy has a greater potential to influence the short-term rate of economic growth than variations in saving. It is possible for the Federal Reserve (Fed) to take steps to prevent any short-run slowdown in economic growth that might result from an increase in the saving rate. That may be especially true in the case of an increase in federal government saving (either an increased surplus or reduced deficit) since there is such a long lead time between enacting a budget and any resulting change in saving.

AN INCREASE IN SAVING: LONG-RUN EFFECTS

As was discussed in the previous section, an increase in domestic saving is likely to result in either an increase in domestic investment or a reduction in borrowing from foreigners. This section discusses how an increase in saving might affect the composition of output, and what that might mean for economic growth.

Increased Investment

If an increase in domestic saving results in more domestic investment and a higher capital-labor ratio, will that raise the long-term rate of growth? The prevailing view of economic theory suggests that the answer to that question, perhaps surprisingly, is that it will not.

In the standard model, growth depends on three factors: growth in the labor force; advances in technology; and growth in the capital stock. The rate of growth of the labor force is assumed to be given and is considered to be independent. Growth in the capital stock depends on the saving rate and the rate at which capital depreciates.

For the sake of clarity and simplicity, consider a hypothetical economy with no technological progress. In the absence of technological progress, the economy will grow at the rate of growth of the labor force. If investment remains a constant share of output, then the capital stock will grow at the same rate as output. Since all three variables grow at the same rate, the ratios of capital to labor and of output to labor are constant as both the numerators and denominators of those ratios are growing at the same rate. This might be referred to as the steady-state rate of growth.

In that steady state, the amount invested will be just enough to replace existing capital as it wears out and to provide for enough new capital through new net investment to ensure that each additional worker in the growing labor force has the same amount of capital to work with as those already employed. In other words, investment is sufficient to maintain a constant capital-to-labor ratio.

Suppose, given these initial conditions, there is a one-time permanent increase in the rate of investment. Each worker now has more capital with which to work, there is a one-time rise in the capital-labor ratio, and the result is a one-time rise in labor productivity. The increase in labor productivity temporarily raises the growth rate of output above that of the labor force.

Only during the transition to the higher rate of investment does the capital stock grow faster than output and the labor force. Furthermore, in this simple example with no technological advance, only during the transition is there an increase in average labor productivity. After the economy adjusts completely to the higher rate of investment, the growth rate of output and the growth rate of the capital stock continue to match the growth rate of the labor force, and the capital-labor ratio is once again constant. **Figure 2** illustrates the point.

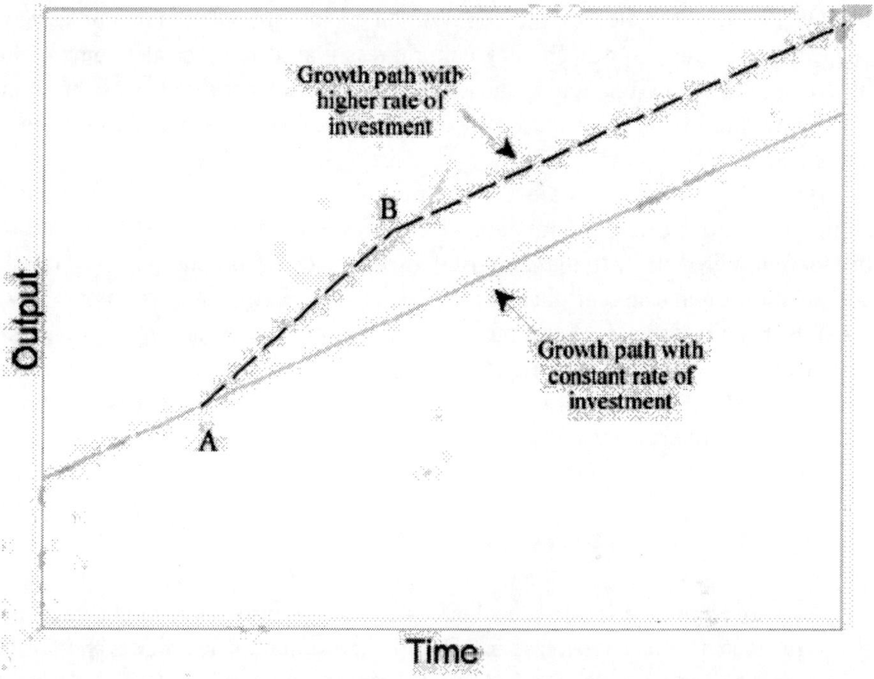

Figure 2. The Effect of Increased Investment on Output

At point ‘A’ in **Figure 2,** there is an increase in the investment share of output. Between points ‘A’ and ‘B,’ the economy adjusts and the ratio of capital to labor rises, and average output per worker also rises. After point ‘B,’ the investment rate is again constant, and the capital stock, the labor force, and total output once again grow at the same rate as before. The only permanent difference is that output is higher than it would have been in the absence of the increase in investment. The long-term rate of growth is unaffected.

Adding technological progress to this simplified model only changes the picture slightly. With technological progress, output and the capital stock grow more rapidly than does the labor force. That means the capital labor ratio rises steadily even with a constant rate of investment. If the rate of investment rises, the rate of increase of the capital-labor ratio briefly accelerates as the economy adjusts. Ultimately, though, the long-term growth rate is determined by the growth of the labor force and the rate of technological progress and is unaffected by the rate of investment.

As with most simple models, there are additional considerations. While the long-term rate of economic growth may be independent of the rate of investment, it may not be unaffected by the composition of investment. Some studies have suggested that the rate of technological progress may depend on the composition of investment spending. Among those types of investments that have been found to be correlated with faster rates of economic growth are education and business equipment.[9]

A number of recent studies has found a connection between investment in computers and other "information technology" equipment and the rate of productivity growth.[10] If the long-run growth rate of output depends on the composition of investment, then it may be that the particular investments made possible by an increase in the rate of investment may be as important as the increase in the rate itself. Moreover, gains to output made possible by redirecting existing levels of investment may be comparable to those gains deriving from an increase in the overall level of investment.

Reduced Imports of Foreign Capital

As was already discussed, an increase in domestic saving might have two consequences. One is an increase in domestic investment. The other is an increase in net exports, and a reduction in U.S. dependence on foreign capital to finance domestic investment.

GDP, the most widely used measure of the size of the U.S. economy and its growth rate, measures the total value of goods and services produced within the nation's borders. The workers producing those goods and services may or may not be U.S. citizens, and the capital stock may be foreign or American owned. To the extent that the domestic capital stock is foreign owned, income produced by that capital will be paid to foreign investors. If an increase in saving does not lead to increased domestic investment, then it will reduce the share of the capital stock that is owned by foreigners.[11]

It isn't only physical capital that is subject to foreign ownership, but any marketable security. That includes federal debt. An increase in domestic saving would also tend to reduce sales to foreigners of federal government debt. Either domestic savers would buy a larger share of new debt issues, or if the increase in saving is attributable to a reduction in federal borrowing, there would simply be less debt for foreigners to buy.

In either case, an increase in domestic saving would reduce foreign investors' claims on income (dividends, interest, and rent) from domestic production. That would leave a larger share of income for Americans. The effect would be similar to that of an increase in investment on domestic output, except instead of an increase in production it would be an increase in income.

POLICY CONSIDERATIONS

Although, from a macroeconomic perspective, it makes little difference who saves, how much is saved does have an effect. As with most policy choices, there are benefits and costs associated with raising the nation's saving rate. But the benefits and costs do not occur at the same time. The benefits of a higher saving rate are long-term in nature, while the cost of saving more is immediate. There may also be a conflict if policymakers decide to use spending and tax policy to stimulate economic growth. In that case, the immediate result would likely be a decline in saving, but any cost associated with a lower saving rate would be incurred in the long run. If policy succeeds in raising national saving, it is likely to be because of an increased appreciation of the long-run benefits

End Notes

[1] For current estimates of saving rates, see CRS Report RS21480, *Saving Rates in the United States: Calculation and Comparison*, by Brian W. Cashell.

[2] For further discussion, see CRS Report RL32119, *Can Public Policy Raise the Saving Rate?*, by Brian W. Cashell.

[3] The discussion that follows will suggest that the actual multiplier is substantially less than four.

[4] Or, where saving is in the form of debt reduction, the supply of financial assets falls.

[5] Martin Feldstein and Charles Horioka, "Domestic Saving and International Capital Flows," *The Economic Journal*, June 1980, pp. 314-329.

[6] Maurice Obstfeld and Alan M. Taylor, *Globalization and Capital Markets*, NBER, Working Paper 8846, March 2002.

[7] Ralph C. Bryant et al., eds, Empirical *Macroeconomics for Interdependent Economies* (Washington: The Brookings Institution, 1988), 342 pp.

[8] Roberto Perotti, *Estimating the Effects of Fiscal Policy in OECD Countries*, paper presented at the "Federal Reserve Bank of San Francisco Conference on Fiscal and Monetary Policy," March 4-5, 2005, 59 pp. Also, Olivier Blanchard and Roberto Perotti, *An Empirical Characterization of*

the Dynamic Effects of Changes in Government Spending and Taxes on Output, NBER ,Working Paper 7269, July 1999.

[9] For an overview of the arguments that the rate of economic growth may depend on a variety of factors see David M. Gould and Roy Ruffin, “What Determines Economic Growth?,” Federal Reserve Bank of Dallas *Economic Review*, second quarter 1993, pp. 25- 40.

[10] Stephen D. Oliner and Daniel E. Sichel, “The Resurgence of Growth in the Late 1990s: Is Information Technology the Story?,” *The Journal of Economic Perspectives*, fall 2000, vol. 14, no. 2, pp. 3-22.

[11] See CRS Report RS21409, *The Budget Deficit and the Trade Deficit: What is Their Relationship?*, by Marc Labonte and Gail Makinen.

In: Savings in the U.S.: Effects, Issues … ISBN: 978-1-60741-357-8
Editor: Lyman T. Randolph

Chapter 3

Why Is the Household Saving Rate So Low?

Brian W. Cashell

Summary

Despite mostly favorable economic conditions since the early 1990s, one development — the focus of this report — may be cause for concern. While the economy was growing, household saving fell to next to nothing. At the beginning of the 1990s, households saved, on average, about 8% of their after-tax income. Since then, it has steadily declined, and since 2005, the proportion of income households set aside has been near zero.

One of the most striking aspects of the economic expansion of the 1990s was the dramatic rise in equity prices. Between 1991 and 2001, the Standard and Poor's index of 500 stock prices rose by 217%, and the NASDAQ stock price index increased by 313%. The standard economic model of saving behavior assumes that households are likely to spend more and save less out of current income given an increase in their wealth. Given that, it seems reasonable to suppose that those increases in equity prices had something to do with the decline in the personal saving rate. A number of studies have found that the decline in the personal saving rate during the 1990s was due at least in part to the rise in equity prices.

The stock market peaked in the second half of 2000. Between September 2000 and October 2002, the S&P 500 fell by 46%. Since then, S&P 500 stock prices have recovered, but they remained slightly below the 2000 peak at the end of 2006. Even though the stock market boom ended, the household saving rate continued to decline. The fact that household saving continued to be anemic even after the stock market cooled suggests that there are other factors that need to be considered. One candidate is the boom in the housing market. Since late 1997, the price of housing has risen rapidly. Between late 1997 and late 2006, house prices doubled, on average. Although there are reasons to think that housing price appreciation might not be a good substitute for saving, a number of empirical studies, while not quite a consensus, found evidence to suggest that it might.

When changes in personal wealth are taken into account, the decline in the official saving measure may be less of an issue, although there will always be concerns about the durability of any gains in asset prices. With respect to the household sector's contribution to total national saving, that has clearly fallen. Meanwhile, investment spending has risen relative to gross domestic product (GDP), in spite of the decline in personal saving, due to the increase in capital inflows from abroad. Some of the productivity gains likely to result from that increased investment, however, will benefit foreign rather than domestic investors. If house price appreciation slows for a long time, households may end up with less wealth than they anticipate. That would make the current low saving rate seem more of a problem.

This report will be updated as developments warrant.

INTRODUCTION

With the exception of a contraction in 2001, the economy has experienced healthy economic growth since the early 1990s, aided in part by a pickup in productivity growth that began in 1995. At the same time, even in a period of relatively rapid growth in output, inflation remained low. One development however, and the focus of this report, may be cause for concern. While the economy was growing, household saving fell to almost nothing. At the beginning of the 1990s, households saved, on average, about 8% of their after-tax income. Since then, it has steadily declined, and since 2005, the proportion of income households set aside has been near zero.

A negative saving rate would seem to be cause for worry. Congress has already indicated its desire to promote household saving by, among other things, creating individual retirement accounts, and saving is an important consideration in proposals to reform Social Security.

Household saving is important for two distinct reasons. First, most households must accumulate wealth over the course of their working lives if they are to avoid a decline in their standard of living after retiring. Saving next to nothing would seem unlikely to afford a comfortable retirement for many, especially if Social Security benefits are ever reduced as part of any reform plan, as many workers fear may occur. Second, households are an important source of funds to finance capital investment, increasing the capital stock and adding to worker productivity.

This paper begins by showing how much the household saving rate has declined in recent years. Next, it explains how household saving is measured, and provides some detail on how saving varies across the income distribution. Finally, it discusses factors that may account for the decline in household saving, as well as how much of a policy concern the decline in household saving may be.[1]

THE DECLINE IN HOUSEHOLD SAVING

The personal, or household, saving rate has fallen steadily since 1990. Personal saving as a percentage of after tax personal income fell from just under 8% in 1990 to near zero since 2005. **Figure 1** shows the monthly personal saving rate since 1970.

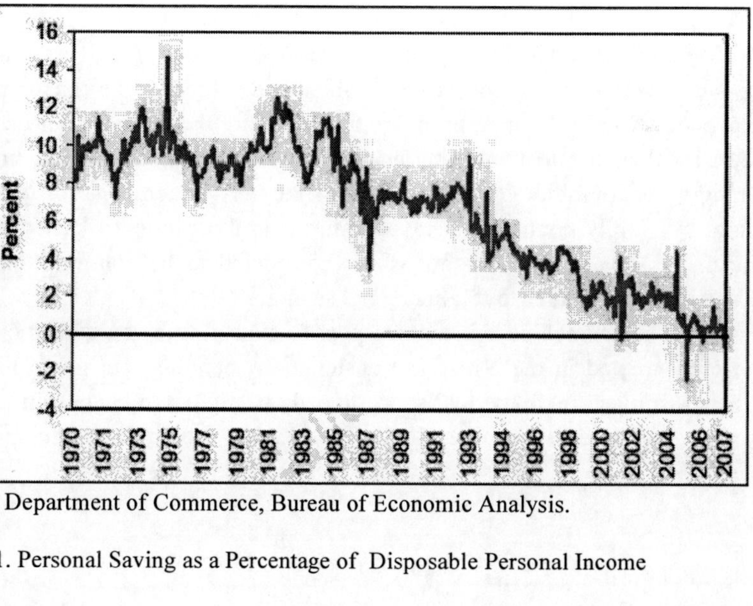

Source: Department of Commerce, Bureau of Economic Analysis.

Figure 1. Personal Saving as a Percentage of Disposable Personal Income

Clearly the personal saving rate has dropped. But it is important to understand what, exactly, this measure of saving takes into account. As is the case with many economic statistics, there are differences between the theoretical notion of saving and statistical efforts to measure it.

MEASURING SAVING

The simplest definition of saving is income minus consumption. But what counts as income and how to measure consumption can be complicated. The national income and product accounts (NIPA) published by the Bureau of Economic Analysis (BEA) of the Department of Commerce are the primary source for statistics on overall U.S. economic activity.[2] The aim of the NIPA is to account for both income and expenditures that are related to the current production of goods and services. Changes in asset values are not included since they have nothing to do with current production. Thus, capital gains and losses are not counted as income in the NIPA.

Even though capital gains are not included in the NIPA measure of personal income, they still affect the measurement of the personal saving rate. Tax payments on capital gains realizations are included in personal tax payments. Thus, after-tax personal income is reduced by the amount of the tax payments. Saving, which is calculated by subtracting consumption from income, is reduced as well.

A difference between saving in a theoretical sense and the NIPA measure of saving is in the treatment of consumer durable goods.[3] Ideally, the consumption of durable goods would be measured by the value of the flow of services they provide over their useful lives, similar to an investment. In the NIPA, however, consumption of durable goods is treated like any other type of consumer spending, by simply counting the expenditures on those goods. That portion of income that is invested in housing is not considered to be consumption in the NIPA and thus contributes to total personal saving.[4]

A similar difference occurs with respect to expenditures on education. They are currently treated in the NIPA as consumption spending, but given that they yield benefits over an individual's lifetime they might more appropriately be counted as investment spending. If they were, that would raise the measured saving rate.

An Alternative Measure

The Board of Governors of the Federal Reserve Board (Fed) publishes an estimate of household saving that differs somewhat from the one published by BEA. The BEA estimate of household saving is calculated by subtracting consumption expenditures from income. In contrast, the Fed estimate is based on a balance sheet for the household sector. When households save, it shows up in the Fed's flow of funds accounts as an increase in household net worth. The gross increase in household net worth is the sum of the net acquisition of financial and tangible assets minus the net increase in household liabilities.

Using net acquisition of tangible assets to measure saving means that not only is investment in housing included in the flow of funds measure of saving, but also net investment in consumer durable goods. Since consumer spending on durable goods is substantial, including it in the flow of funds measure of saving means that the Fed's estimate of household saving is usually higher than BEA's estimate. **Figure 2** shows the household saving rate from the flow of funds accounts including the net increase in household durable goods. The alternative Fed measure shows the same steady decline in the household saving rate beginning in the 1980s as the BEA measure. But instead of falling from about 10% to below zero, the Fed measure shows a decline from about 14% to about zero.

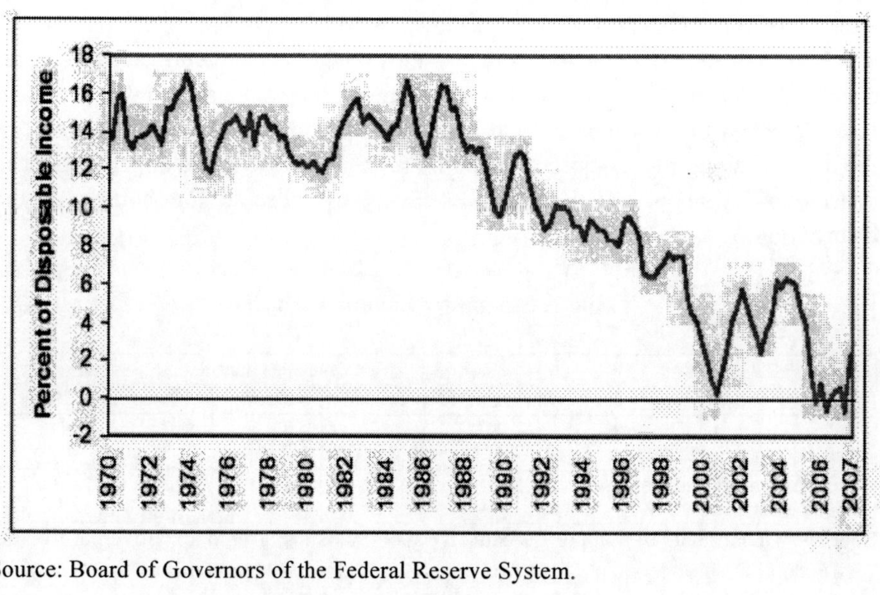

Source: Board of Governors of the Federal Reserve System.

Figure 2. Flow of Funds Household Saving Rate

Accounting for net investment in consumer durables as saving is entirely appropriate given that saving is defined as income less consumption. But when policymakers express concern about the low saving rate the distinction between the Fed measure and the BEA measure may not be very significant. The public policy concern over low household saving is one related to retirement saving, and investments in automobiles and household furnishings are not likely to be a source of income for retirees. What is significant is that the independent measures both show that household saving has fallen to very low historical levels.

Who Saves?

The saving rates depicted in **Figures 1** and **2** are averages. But not everyone saves at the same rate and it might be more informative to have an idea of how saving rates vary across households, by income in particular. **Table 1** presents data on saving by quintile of income. The lowest quintile represents the bottom 20% of the income distribution, the second quintile represents the second lowest 20% in the distribution, and so on. The figures in the first row show saving rates.[5] They are derived from data from the 2006 Survey of Consumer Expenditures, published by the Bureau of Labor Statistics. The figures in the second row are taken from the 2004 Survey of Consumer Finances published by the Board of Governors of the Federal Reserve System.[6]

Both sets of numbers indicate that those at the upper end of the income distribution account for most saving. On average, they save at a higher rate than those lower in the distribution, and a larger proportion of them save. Given that the overall saving rate is close to zero, the saving of those at the upper end of the distribution is about equal to the dis-saving of those at the bottom of the distribution.

Table 1. Saving by Income Quintile

	Income Quintile				
	Lowest	**Second**	**Third**	**Fourth**	**Fifth**
Saving as a percent of aftertax household income (2006)	-104.7	-14.7	5.4	18.7	33.6
Percentage of families that saved (2004)	34.0	43.5	54.4	69.3	79.2

Sources: Department of Labor, Bureau of Labor Statistics; Board of Governors of the Federal Reserve System.

HOUSEHOLD SAVING AND RETIREMENT

The standard model of consumer spending used in economic analysis makes the basic assumption that consumers seek to avoid large swings in their living standards over the course of their lifetimes. Thus as incomes rise and fall both in the short and long term, individuals are expected to vary their saving rate in order to minimize the effect on their consumption.

Typically, over the course of an individual's lifetime, income has a tendency first to rise over the course of a career, and then fall in retirement. The model of saving based on this "life cycle" presumes that, in order to dampen the effects of the lifetime income cycle on consumption and living standards, individuals vary the rate at which they save. Saving will thus tend to be relatively higher during their peak earning years, and lower at the beginning of their careers and during retirement.

From an economic perspective, there is no "ideal" saving rate. The rate at which an individual saves is, for the most part, simply a reflection of his willingness to consume less now in order to be able to consume more in the future. Taking the life cycle model as a guide, however, prudent individuals might be expected to save enough to avoid a substantial decline in their living standard on retirement.

If consumers do seek to maintain a fairly stable level of consumption over their entire lives, then the level of consumption at any given point in their lives will depend on their current wealth and some expectation about their earnings over the rest of their lives.[7]

There are a number of implications that follow this model of consumer behavior. One is that an unexpected one-time income windfall is more likely to be saved than spent. A rise in income that is temporary is less likely to raise consumption than one that is permanent as long as consumers seek to maintain a relatively constant standard of living. A permanent increase in income is more likely to induce an increase in consumption, so that the saving rate will be less affected. Similarly, an increase in overall wealth raises consumption possibilities over the long run. An increase in wealth that is believed to be permanent will tend to raise consumption. Unless there is a corresponding increase in income, an increase in wealth is likely to reduce the measured rate of saving.

Consumption is ultimately constrained by income and wealth. An increase in wealth increases potential lifetime consumption and diminishes an individual's incentive to save. The effect of an increase in wealth on consumption and saving may depend on a number of variables. Most important, if the life cycle model is correct, only a fraction of any increase in wealth would affect current consumption because any rise in consumption would be spread out over one's remaining lifetime. Some increases in wealth may not be viewed as permanent as might be the case with assets whose prices tend to be highly variable. If there is uncertainty about the permanence of an increase in wealth then it is less likely to affect consumption and saving. In addition, a strong desire to leave a bequest may dampen the influence increasing wealth has on consumption.

Numerous studies of wealth and consumer spending have been conducted. Empirical estimates of the magnitude of the effect of changes in wealth on consumption vary, but they tend to be fairly small. The estimates suggest that for each additional dollar of wealth, consumption spending tends to rise by anywhere from 1 cent to 7 cents.[8]

Equity Prices and Personal Saving

One of the most striking aspects of the economic expansion of the 1990s was the dramatic rise in equity prices. Between 1991, the beginning of the expansion, and 2001, the year it ended, the Standard and Poor's index of 500 stock prices rose by 217%, the Dow Jones Index rose by 247%, and the NASDAQ stock price index increased by 313%. Given the model of saving behavior described above, it seems reasonable to suppose that those increases in equity prices had something to do with the coincidental decline in the personal saving rate.

A number of studies have found that the decline in the personal saving rate during the 1990s was due at least in part to the rise in equity prices. Lusardi, Skinner, and Venti found that between one-half to two-thirds of the decline in the personal saving rate was attributable to the effect of wealth gains on consumption spending.[9] They also point out that because of rising equity prices, firms were able to reduce their contributions to defined benefit retirement plans and still keep those plans fully funded. Pension benefits could be paid out of the capital gains of the pension fund. That tended to reduce a component of personal income (employers' contributions to pension funds) without reducing consumption and thus contributed to the decline in the saving rate.

Maki and Palumbo analyzed the drop in saving of the 1990s and found that almost all of it could be attributed to the performance of the stock market.[10] Moreover, they found that those households with the highest incomes experienced the largest gains in wealth and also the largest declines in saving rates. In fact, they found that, between 1992 and 2000, almost all of the decline in the aggregate personal saving rate can be attributed to reduced saving of those households in the top 20% of the income distribution. They also found that the saving rate of those households in the bottom 40% of the income distribution actually rose over the same period.

It seems both theoretically and empirically clear that the large increase in equity prices of the 1990s likely had something to do with the decline in the measured rate of personal saving. If the drop in saving was simply a response to the increase in asset values, then households at the end of the 1990s were not necessarily any less well prepared for the future than if stock prices had not risen so rapidly and the saving rate had not fallen. In this sense existing measures of personal saving may not be very good guides to the extent to which individuals are preparing for retirement or the proverbial rainy day.

Because capital gains can contribute just as much as saving to a household's retirement nest egg, it might be appropriate to include them in any measure of retirement saving. After all, the aim of saving for retirement is to accumulate enough wealth to be able to continue, in retirement, the lifestyle to which one has become accustomed during one's working life. Gale and Sabelhaus have calculated what the saving rate might have been if capital gains were included in the current measure of personal saving.[11] They found that, after adjusting for inflation, household wealth rose at least as rapidly in the late 1990s as at any time since 1960.

Until the end of 2000, this explanation for the decline in the saving rate was widely accepted. But subsequent developments suggested that stock price movements alone are insufficient to explain the downward trend in household saving.

House Prices and Saving

The stock market peaked in the second half of 2000. Between September 2000 and October 2002, the S&P 500 index of stock prices fell by 46%. Since then, stock prices have recovered, but they remained slightly below the 2000 peak at the beginning of 2008. Even though the stock market boom ended, the household saving rate continued to decline.

Much of the wealth gain due to the equity appreciation of the 1990s endures, but it was the appreciation that allowed households to accumulate wealth without saving out of current income. If rising equity prices in the 1990s are the explanation for declining household saving, then household saving might have been expected to rise when the stock market declined during 2001 and 2002. But that did not happen.

The fact that household saving continued to be anemic even after the stock market cooled suggests that there are other factors that need to be considered. One candidate is the boom in the housing market. Since late 1997, the price of housing has risen rapidly relative to prior years. Between late 1997 and late 2007, the house price index published by the Office of Federal Housing Enterprise Oversight (OFHEO) doubled.

There are reasons it might seem less likely that an increase in the value of houses would have the same effect on household saving behavior as equity price appreciation. An increase in house prices increases the wealth of current homeowners, but it also increases the cost of housing. For renters, that might result in a reduction in saving in order to pay increased rents. For many homeowners, an increase in housing wealth may simply translate into an increase in consumption of housing, rather than spending more for other goods and services. In that case, an increase in housing prices would be unlikely to show up as a reduction in saving out of current income.

Another consideration is that some savers may have a bequest motive for saving. In other words, they save more than is necessary for their own well-being in retirement in order to be able to pass some wealth on to their children. A permanent increase in the price of housing now would also increase its cost for future generations. Presumably, many of those for whom the bequest motive is important would increase their desired bequest to compensate for the higher cost of housing.

It may also be more difficult for homeowners to consume any of the gains from house price appreciation. Transaction costs in the housing market are significantly higher than they are in equity markets, although homeowners may be able to borrow against any gains they have. It has also been suggested that because of the perceived illiquidity of housing wealth homeowners have no expectation of being able to consume out of capital gains in housing.

A number of studies have found that the effect on saving of asset price appreciation depends on the kind of asset. For example, Juster, et al., found that for each $1 increase in wealth, household spending rose (saving fell) by about 3 cents.[12] But they also found that the effect of asset price appreciation on spending depended on the type of asset. They found that household spending was much more influenced by gains in equity wealth than was the case for any other type of asset.

The authors found a large effect on saving of appreciation in stock prices, as much as 19 cents for each dollar gain in equity wealth. But the effect of house price appreciation was much smaller. The effect of a $1 increase in housing wealth was a 3 cent drop in saving, but the estimate was not statistically significant. While the increase in equity prices during the 1990s may explain the drop in household saving, this study suggests the rise in house values is an unlikely reason for the saving rate's continued decline.

Other studies, however, have suggested that housing price appreciation may have had a significant effect on household saving. Belsky and Prakken found that in the long run, the effects on household saving of house and equity price variations were similar.[13] They also found that house price appreciation had a more immediate effect and that the effect of equity price appreciation took longer to be fully reflected in the saving rate. The authors suggested that may be because historically equity prices have been more volatile than house prices, and so households may be more confident in the durability of house price gains. The authors also indicated that the strong effect of the post-2000 boom in house prices may have been partly due to the simultaneous decline in interest rates which encouraged homeowners to refinance as well as borrow. They left open the question of whether, in other circumstances, house price appreciation would have the same effect on household saving.

Case, et al., did a cross-country and cross-state comparison of changes in both housing and equity wealth and the effect on household spending.[14] They found that increases in housing wealth had a greater effect on household spending (and, hence, saving) than increases in equity wealth. They also found evidence that the correlation between increases in housing wealth and spending increased after 1986 when tax law changes made it more advantageous for households to borrow against home equity.

Benjamin, et al., found that changes in real estate wealth had a greater effect on spending and saving than variations in financial wealth.[15] The authors found that for each $1 increase in real estate wealth household saving would fall by 8 cents, while for each $1 increase in financial wealth household saving would fall by just 2 cents. They suggest that the effect of variations in financial wealth might be smaller because much financial wealth is tied up in pension and insurance funds and gains are not easy to withdraw. They also point out that financial wealth is concentrated and that some financial asset holding may represent controlling interests in businesses and thus not readily liquidated.

Although there are reasons to think that housing price appreciation might not be a substitute for saving, the empirical studies, while not quite amounting to a consensus, found evidence to suggest that it might. The recent decline in house prices might begin the pose a problem if it proves to be more than temporary and there is no offsetting increase in household saving.

Other Considerations

In addition to equity and housing price appreciation, the recent sharp rise in energy prices has also been offered as an explanation for some of the decline in household saving.[16] But if energy prices do not decline from recent highs that explanation does not alleviate concerns for the long run.

Accounting issues have also been suggested as possible reasons for the decline in measured saving. In particular, the fact that stock repurchases are not counted as part of personal income may have caused both income and saving to be understated. There has been an increase in stock repurchases in recent years.[17]

Clearly, there is no shortage of potential explanations for the decline in household saving. A recent study published by the St. Louis Federal Reserve Bank reviewed all of the potential explanations and came to the conclusion that while each of them may have its merits, none of them is compelling and that much of the decline in saving remained a puzzle.[18]

Are Households Saving Enough?

Even if the decline in the saving rate could be explained, it does not answer the question of whether Americans are saving enough, or accumulating enough wealth, to avoid experiencing a decline in their living standard in retirement. One study attempted to estimate how much households should be setting aside in order to maintain their living standards into retirement.[19] Using a retirement planning financial model and data from a survey of the financial status of households approaching retirement, it was found that low-income households (those with incomes below $15,000) needed to save only about 1% of their income. But that assumed that there would be no cuts in Social Security benefits. When it is assumed that Social Security benefits are cut by 30% in 15 years, the desired saving rate rises to 6%.

Households that have higher incomes need to save at higher rates if they are to avoid a decline in their living standards on retirement, because Social Security benefits will account for a much smaller share of their retirement income. The desired saving rate for those households with incomes between $15,000 and $100,000 was about 14%, but rose to about 20% when it was assumed that future Social Security benefits would be cut.

CONCLUSION

The drop in personal saving that occurred over the past 15 years may not be as troubling as might first appear, at least with respect to retirement planning, for several reasons. The decline in personal saving coincided with large increases in equity values and housing wealth. When changes in personal wealth are taken into account, the decline in the official saving measure may be less of an issue, although there will always be concerns about the durability of any gains in asset prices. With respect to the household sector's contribution to total national saving, that has clearly fallen. Meanwhile investment spending has risen relative to gross domestic product (GDP), in spite of the decline in personal saving, due to the increase in capital inflows from abroad. Some of the productivity gains likely to result from that increased investment, however, will benefit foreign rather than domestic investors.[20]

While the low saving rate may not pose an immediate economic risk, there could be significant consequences if it persists. Households apparently felt a diminishing need to save out of current income during the 1990s because of the large increase in stock prices. Stock prices have since declined, but house price appreciation seems to have encouraged households to save even less.

An additional consideration is that the large federal government surpluses of the late 1990s have now evaporated. For the immediate future, the federal government will continue spending more than it is taking in, which means that the public sector saving rate will be much lower than it was in the late 1990s. Without an increase in household or business saving, either investment spending must fall, or the United States will have to continue importing substantial amounts of capital from abroad.

If foreigners were to reduce or stop their investments in the United States, then the decline in demand for U.S. financial assets would cause their prices to fall and interest rates would rise. Without an offsetting increase in domestic saving, the rise in interest rates would be likely to result in a decline in domestic investment.

End Notes

1 For a complete accounting of saving in the United States, see CRS Report RS21480, *Saving Rates in the United States: Calculation and Comparison*, by Brian W. Cashell.

2 This is the source for the data shown in **Figure 1**.

3 Consumer durable goods consist mainly of purchases of automobiles, furniture, and household equipment.

[4] Marshall B. Reinsdorf, "Alternative Measures of Saving," *Survey of Current Business,* September 2004, pp. 17-27.

[5] These saving rates should not be taken as precise estimates. They are derived by subtracting expenditures from income as reported in a survey. If the estimates of income and expenditures are biased in opposite directions then there could be considerable error in the resulting saving estimate.

[6] This survey is conducted every three years.

[7] To the extent that consumers can borrow against future income, that enhances their ability to maintain a fairly steady level of consumption over a long period of time.

[8] See Martha Starr-McCluer, "Stock Market Wealth and Consumer Spending," Finance and Economics Discussion Series, 1998-20, Board of Governors of the Federal Reserve System, April 1998, 21 pp. Also, Congressional Budget Office, *The Economic and Budget Outlook: An Update*, August 1998, p. 19.

[9] Annamaria Lusardi, Jonathan Skinner, and Steven Venti, "Saving Puzzles and Saving Policies in the United States," National Bureau of Economic Research, Working Paper 8237, April 2001, 52 pp.

[10] Dean M. Maki and Michael G. Palumbo, "Disentangling the Wealth Effect: A Cohort Analysis of Household Saving in the 1990s," Board of Governors of the Federal Reserve System, Finance and Economics Discussion Series, 2001-21, April 2001, 38 pp.

[11] William G. Gale and John Sabelhaus, "The Savings Crisis: In the Eye of the Beholder?" *The Milken Institute Review*, Third Quarter 1999, pp. 46-56.

[12] F. Thomas Juster, Joseph P. Lupton, James P. Smith, and Frank Stafford, *The Decline in Household Saving and the Wealth Effect*, Board of Governors of the Federal Reserve System Working Paper 2004-31, June 2004, 17 pp.

[13] Eric Belsky and Joel Prakken, "Housing's Impact on Wealth Accumulation, Wealth Distribution and Consumer Spending," National Association of Realtors National Center for Real Estate Research, 2004, 26 pp.

[14] Karl E. Case, John M. Quigley, and Robert J. Shiller, "Comparing Wealth Effects: The Stock Market versus the Housing Market," Institute of Business and Economic Research, University of California, Berkeley, Working Paper W01-004, 2005, 32 pp.

[15] John D. Benjamin, Peter Chinloy, and G. Donald Jud, "Real Estate Versus Financial Wealth in Consumption," *Journal of Real Estate Finance and Economics*, vol. 29, no. 3, 2004, pp. 341-354.

[16] Charles Steindel, "How Worrisome Is a Negative Saving Rate?," Federal Reserve Bank of New York, *Current Issues in Economics and Finance*, May 2007, 7 pp.

[17] Ibid.

[18] Massimo Guidolin and Elizabeth A. La Jeunesse, "The Decline in the U.S. Personal Saving Rate: Is It Real and Is It a Puzzle?, Federal Reserve Bank of St. Louis *Review*, vol. 89, no. 6 (November/December 2007), pp. 491-514.

[19] B. Douglas Bernheim, Lorenzo Forni, Jagadeesh Gokhale, and Laurence J. Kotlikoff, "How Much Should Americans Be Saving for Retirement?," Federal Reserve Bank of Cleveland Working Paper 00-02, January 1999, 13 pp.

[20] See CRS Report RL33140, *Is the U.S. Trade Deficit Caused by a Global Saving Glut?*, by Marc Labonte.

In: Savings in the U.S.: Effects, Issues ... ISBN: 978-1-60741-357-8
Editor: Lyman T. Randolph

Chapter 4

SAVING INCENTIVES: WHAT MAY WORK, WHAT MAY NOT

Thomas L. Hungerford

SUMMARY

Saving is the portion of national output that is not consumed and represents resources that can be used to increase, replace, or improve the nation's capital stock. The U.S. net national saving rate reached a post-war peak of 12.4% in 1965 and has then trended downward since to a low of 1.9% in 2006. Many analysts claim that saving is too low. Among the Organization for Economic Cooperation and Development (OECD) countries, the United States has the third lowest saving rate.

Survey evidence suggests that people know why they should save, but many don't save, especially lower-income individuals and families. Several reasons have been offered to explain the declining personal saving rate and the relatively high proportion of individuals and families that do not save. Economic reasons start from the premise that individuals and families are rational and make optimal decisions about consumption and saving throughout the life course. Low saving rates are then explained by economic disincentives induced by government policy or by life cycle changes in the propensity to save. Behavioral reasons start from the premise that individuals and families do not always make optimal decisions regarding consumption and saving.

The government offers tax incentives to individuals and families to save. The empirical evidence on the relationship of tax incentives to the saving rate mostly comes from examinations of traditional individual retirement accounts (IRAs) and 401(k) plans. The reported results are mixed, but generally indicate small effects. Be that as it may, the tax incentives tend to benefit higher-income individuals and families to a much greater extent than lower-income individuals and families. The primary reasons are (1) higher-income individuals are much more likely to save, and (2) higher-income individuals face higher marginal tax rates and benefit more from sheltering income from taxation.

Furthermore, the tax revenue loss for these incentives lower public saving by reducing the budget surplus or increasing the budget deficit. For FY2007, these tax incentives are estimated to cost the U.S. Treasury $133.8 billion in forgone tax revenues — almost 85% of the estimated FY2007 budget deficit. The Bush Administration and the President's Advisory Panel on Federal Tax Reform have advocated expanding tax incentives as the primary policy to encourage personal saving. Research has shown that personal saving has been fairly unresponsive to tax incentives, however, and such incentives may substantially decrease public saving (that is, increase the budget deficit). The long-term net effect on national saving and economic growth is likely negative.

This report contains historical data and will not be updated.

From an individual's perspective, saving is "money in the bank." The increases in wealth that saving represents can be spent in the near future for emergencies or children's educational expenses, in the distant future for retirement, or passed down to heirs.[1] From a national perspective, however, saving is income that is not spent on consumption goods or services. That is, it is the portion of national output that is not consumed and represents resources that can be used to increase, replace, or improve the nation's capital stock.[2]

Many analysts claim that saving is too low. For example, recent research has shown that about a quarter of the U.S. population live in households whose assets are below 25% of the poverty threshold.[3] If housing wealth is not included, the proportion increases to over 40% of the U.S. population. Furthermore, retirement specialists argue that many people nearing retirement have not accumulated enough assets to maintain their present living standards after retirement.[4]

At the national level, analysts caution against a low savings rate. They argue that high capital investment is a good thing, but if it is not financed by national saving it has to be financed by borrowing abroad.[5] Persistent borrowing from abroad builds up international liabilities and implies increasing shares of national income will be sent overseas as interest and dividends. It is difficult to say that the U.S. national saving rate is too low since there is no universally accepted definition of what constitutes a low saving rate. But it is noteworthy that among the Organization for Economic Cooperation and Development (OECD) countries, the United States has the third lowest saving rate.[6]

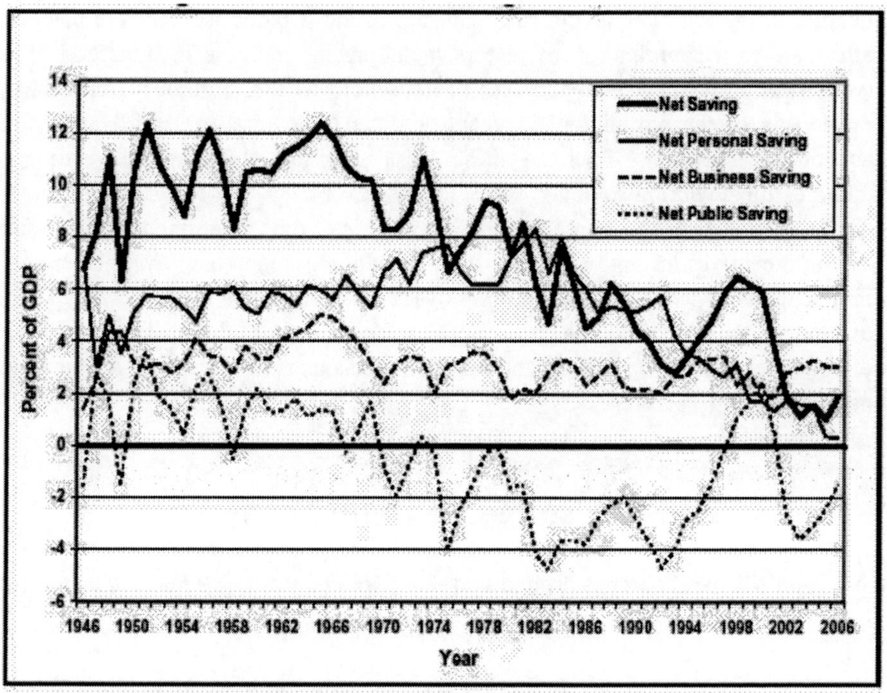

Source: Department of Commerce, Bureau of Economic Analysis.

Figure 1. Net National Saving Rates, 1946-2006

The post-World War II trend in the U.S. saving rate (saving as a percentage of gross domestic product) is shown in **Figure 1**.[7] The net national saving rate (the heavy solid line) reached a post-war peak of 12.4% in 1965 and has trended downward since then to a low of 1.9% in 2006.

There are three components to national saving. The first is personal saving or the saving by individuals and households (the light solid line in the figure). This is what people typically think of as saving. The second component is business saving, which consists of corporate retained earnings (the dashed line). The final component is public saving, which is federal, state, and local government surpluses (the dotted line). Public saving can be and often is negative if the government sector is running a deficit.

The decline in the national saving rate since 1965 has two main sources. First, the public saving rate fell from 1.4% in 1965 to -4.2% in 1983. Most of this decline in the public saving rate was due to increasing federal budget deficits. After 1982, the steady fall in the personal saving rate accounts for much of the decline in the national saving rate. The fall in the personal saving rate has been attributed to a combination of factors including the increase in transfer income (which is rarely saved), an increase in household wealth, and an increase in the proportion of the population 65 years or older (who tend to spend rather than accumulate savings).[8] Each of these could increase consumption relative to income, thus lowering saving.

In response to the perceived low saving rate, the government offers many saving incentives through the tax system. In addition, many employers offer some inducements to encourage their employees to save for retirement. This report examines why individuals and households save or don't save, and the effectiveness of the various incentives and inducements in increasing personal and national saving.

Reasons for Saving and Not Saving

John Maynard Keynes argued that there are eight primary reasons or motives leading individuals to save (that is, to forgo consumption):[9]

Precaution motive: "To build up a reserve against unforeseen contingencies,"
Foresight motive: "To provide for an anticipated future relation between the income and the needs of the individual or his family different from that which exists in the present,"
Calculation motive: "To enjoy interest and appreciation,"
Improvement motive: "To enjoy gradually increasing expenditures,"
Independence motive: "To enjoy a sense of independence and the power to do things,"
Enterprise motive: "To secure a *masse de manœuvre* to carry out speculative or business projects,"
Pride (bequest) motive: "To bequeath a fortune," and
Avarice motive: "To satisfy pure miserliness."

Others have added a down payment motive as a ninth reason for saving.[10] Recent survey evidence generally confirms that many of these motives are the main reasons why Americans save (see **Table 1**). The table reports the response of prime-aged heads of households grouped by age and income.[11]

Table 1. Reasons for Saving by Age and Income Group

	Ages 25-39		Ages 40-49		Ages 50-59	
	Bottom Half	Top Half	Bottom Half	Top Half	Bottom Half	Top Half
Retirement	14.5%	31.1%	30.7%	50.4%	38.1%	48.8%
Precautionary	30.1	30.9	29.8	20.0	31.4	23.0
House	12.9	6.3	6.5	1.4	3.4	2.8
Purchases	9.9	5.1	10.7	4.4	9.8	4.6
Education	20.1	19.4	12.4	21.0	6.4	8.2
Other	9.4	6.8	4.6	1.9	4.4	3.8
Can't Save	3.2	0.4	5.4	1.0	6.6	0.4

Source: CRS tabulation of 2004 Survey of Consumer Finances.
Note: Columns may not sum to 100% due to rounding.

Four major points can be made about these results. First, saving for retirement is generally the most important reason for saving in nearly every age and income group. The foresight or retirement motive is stronger for older age groups — the age groups closer to retirement. Furthermore, families in the upper half of the income distribution are more likely to cite saving for retirement as their primary reason for saving than those in the lower half of the income distribution.

Second, saving for the inevitable rainy day (the precaution motive) appears to be the primary reason for saving among younger families in the lower half of the income distribution. For the other groups, it is the second most frequently cited reason for saving. For the older two age groups, those with lower income are more likely to save for precautionary reasons than those with more income.

Third, within each age group, those in the lower half of the income distribution are more likely than those in the upper half to cite saving for future purchases of goods and services such as homes, home repairs, and durable goods as the most important reason to save. A possible explanation for this disparity by income is lower-income families may be credit constrained and have to save for purchases rather than using a credit card.

Lastly, among the youngest families, about one in five report that education is the most important reason for saving (the improvement motive). For the young families, there is not much difference between the two income groups. Older families, especially those in the oldest age group, are less likely to report this as an important reason for saving since their children are generally grown and finished with their formal education.

The results reported in **Table 1** suggest that people know why they should save, but provides little information on whether or not they do save. **Figure 2** shows the percentage of families in each age and income group who report not saving. There is relatively little variation across age groups — about 20% of the families do not save. There are large disparities, however, by income. About 10% of the families in the upper half of the income distribution report not saving. In contrast, about a third of the families in the lower half of the income distribution do not save.

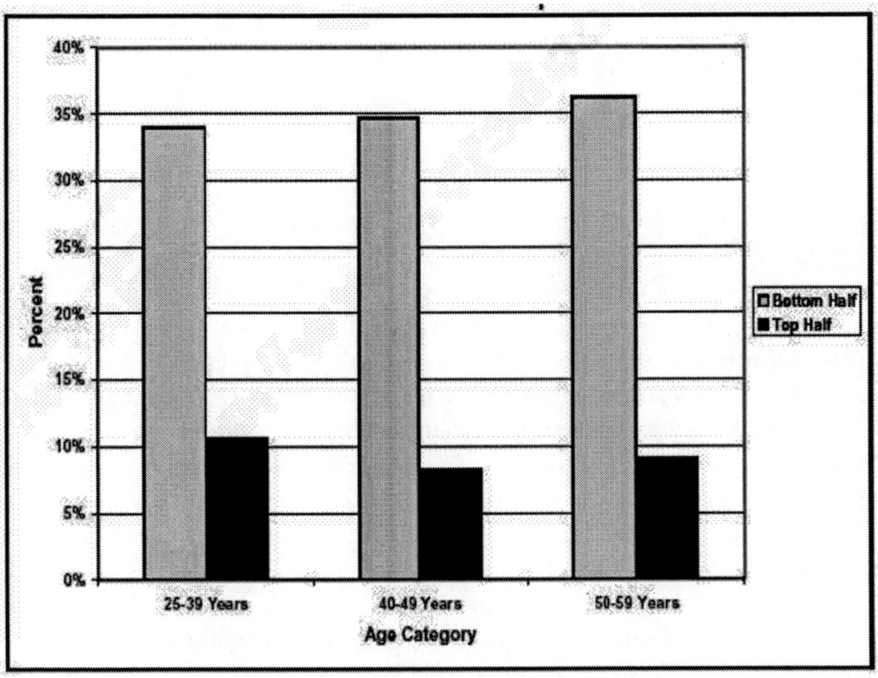

Source: CRS analysis of 2004 Survey of Consumer Finances. Percent

Figure 2. Percentage of Households Not Saving By Age and Income Group

Several reasons have been offered for the declining personal saving rate and the relatively high proportion of individuals and families that do not save. The economic reasons start from the premise that individuals and families are rational and make optimal decisions about consumption and saving throughout the life course. Low saving rates are then explained by economic disincentives induced by government policy or by life cycle changes in the propensity to save. Behavioral reasons start from the premise that individuals and families do not always make optimal decisions regarding consumption and saving.

Economic Reasons for Low Savings and Saving Rates

At the aggregate level, some analysts point out that the rising proportion of the elderly in the U.S. population may explain the declining saving rate. Since the elderly should dissave (that is, spend their savings) rather than save, the aggregate saving rate should fall. Research has shown, however, that saving rates do not vary that much across age groups, and the change in the age distribution in the 1980s was too small to explain the decline in the aggregate saving rate.[12]

Although the change in the age distribution of the U.S. population toward a higher proportion of elderly may not explain the fall in the saving rate, there is evidence that the elderly now are saving less than past cohorts of elderly. Research shows that there has been an increase in annuitization of wealth (especially Social Security and defined benefit pension wealth) which could be due to lessened bequest and precautionary motives.[13] Consequently, consumption by the elderly is higher and saving is lower. More elderly who are saving less may have had some effect on the personal saving rate. But this does not explain low saving rates for younger individuals. Furthermore, this finding may change in the future with the shift from defined benefit pension plans to defined contribution pension plans (especially 401(k) plans), which do not have to be annuitized at retirement.

Some have argued that social welfare programs (social insurance and public assistance) have contributed to the decline in saving. Social insurance programs such as unemployment insurance and Social Security (both for disability and old age) may have reduced the need for precautionary saving.[14] But there have been no large scale changes in these programs since 1980 that could explain the trend in personal saving. Furthermore, recent research shows that the precautionary saving motive does not give rise to much wealth in the economy and probably to relatively little saving.[15]

A related argument suggests that asset-based, means-tested public assistance programs such as Temporary Assistance to Needy Families, Supplemental Security Income, and food stamps discourage saving by families with low expected lifetime earnings. Proponents of this argument point out that the asset test acts as an implicit 100% tax rate on savings "in the event of an earnings downturn or medical expense large enough to cause the household to seek welfare support."[16] This would prevent these families from saving for precautionary reasons and for retirement since most public assistance programs include both regular and retirement savings accounts as assets subject to the asset limit. This may help explain why lower-income families have little savings, but does not explain the decline in the personal saving rate since the mid-1980s because the means-testing rules of these programs have not substantially changed over the past 25 years. In addition, many low-income families do not save because after everyday living expenses are covered there is little or no money left over for saving.

Two financial explanations offered to explain declining saving rates are (1) capital gains in housing and equities, and (2) the development of financial markets. The increase in wealth from unrealized capital gains in housing and equities since 1990 allows individuals and families to maintain a target level of wealth (and even increase the target level) without active saving. The developments and expansion in credit cards and home equity loans mean families do not have to save as much for future durable good and home purchases.

Retirement saving has to last throughout the retirement years. Recent evidence suggests that individuals tend to underestimate how long they will live. Survey results show that a majority of Americans underestimate the life expectancy "for someone their own age and gender."[17] Similarly, British men and women underestimate how long they are likely to live by about five years.[18] Consequently, even if people are saving for retirement, they may be undersaving because they are saving for a shorter retirement period than what they will actually experience. This could help explain low levels of savings, but cannot explain the downward trend in personal saving rates unless there has been a change in Americans' underestimate of their life expectancy.

Behavioral Reasons for Low Savings and Saving Rates

In recent years, behavioral models have been developed to explain low savings and low saving rates, especially for retirement. The traditional economic model of saving, the life-cycle model, assumes that individuals make rational, far-sighted decisions. The theory implies that saving rates increase with age and savings accumulate until retirement when individuals begin to spend down their savings. The bulk of the empirical evidence, however, tends to not support the life-cycle model.[19]

Unlike the traditional economic model for saving, behavioral models stress that individuals can and do make choices that are unfavorable to themselves.

These models emphasize the role of inertia, the lack of self-control, and the limits of human intellectual capabilities.

Retirement savings accounts (for example, 401(k) plans and IRAs) require workers to be proactive and decide to participate, how much to save, and how to invest the retirement account assets. But through inertia, workers may never make or at least postpone making these critical decisions. Research shows that changing the "default" options in 401(k) plans so the workers have to decide not to participate can substantially increase participation rates in these plans and increase retirement saving.[20] Workers, through inertia, also tend to accept the default contribution rate and the investment allocation chosen by the plan administrator. Therefore, the defaults need to be carefully chosen to allow for an adequate return while protecting the worker's investment.

Saving takes will power. Individuals have to forgo current consumption in order to save for future consumption, and they may not have the self-control to forgo consumption.[21] Often individuals develop self-regulatory mechanisms or rules to control spending such as mental accounting systems. In a mental accounting system the individual treats money in different accounts as not being fungible, and has a different propensity to spend money from the different accounts. But equally as often individuals manipulate or bend their own rules of self-control.[22]

To make the complex decisions determining the optimal consumption path over a lifetime requires not only complete information on the economic environment, but also almost unlimited computing power. Individuals, however, rarely have complete information, and may not be able to adequately process the information they do have. To deal with human information processing limitations, individuals often use simple rules of thumb to make these complex decisions and generally accept alternatives that are "good enough" rather than optimal.[23] Consequently, individuals may make seemingly short-sighted decisions and save too little.

Many people nearing retirement age do not plan ahead and have not thought about retirement and financing their retirement. A recent study found that about a third of older Americans aged 50 to 61 years have not thought about retirement. Furthermore, those who have not thought about retirement have significantly lower net financial wealth than those who have thought about retirement (either a little or a lot).[24]

INDUCEMENTS TO SAVE

The government offers various incentives to individuals, families, and businesses to save. In addition, businesses offer a variety of inducements to encourage their employees to save for retirement. The incentives and inducements are designed to overcome one or more barriers to saving.

Tax Incentives

Tax incentives increase the effective rate of return on savings. Tax-favored savings plans for individuals and families are classified as either front-loaded or back-loaded.[25] In front-loaded plans, the contributions are tax deferred so the tax benefits primarily accrue at the time money is contributed to the account. The earnings grow tax-free until the funds are withdrawn or distributed. At that time, both the contributions and earnings are taxed. Traditional deductible IRAs and 401(k) plans are examples of a front-loaded savings accounts. In back-loaded plans, after-tax dollars are contributed to the account, and neither the contributions nor the earnings are taxed for qualified withdrawals. The Roth IRA is the best known example of a back-loaded savings account.

Both types of plans will yield a higher after-tax distribution than regular taxable savings accounts, thus providing an incentive to save in these accounts. As long as the tax rate is the same at the time of withdrawal as when the funds were contributed, both front-loaded and back-loaded savings accounts will yield the same after-tax distribution at retirement. Individuals who save for their children's education, on the one hand, often begin saving early in their working career when their earnings are relatively low, and tend to be in the lower tax brackets. They then withdraw the funds during their peak earning years when their children attend college. Consequently, they may be in a higher tax bracket when the monies are distributed from the savings account. A back-loaded plan may confer greater benefits than a front-loaded plan in this case. On the other hand, individuals saving for retirement often are in higher tax brackets during their working years than at retirement. For these individuals, a front-loaded plan may confer greater benefits. In either case, the saving decisions are often made several years before anticipated withdrawals, and it is difficult to know what tax bracket one will be in so far in advance.

These tax incentives, however, can affect both personal and public saving. The tax revenue loss for these incentives will lower public saving by reducing the budget surplus or increasing the budget deficit.[26] The reduction in public saving may more than offset any increase in personal saving induced by the tax incentives. The costs of front- and back-loaded savings plans are reflected in the federal budget at different times. For front-loaded plans, the tax expenditures are incurred immediately, and the revenues from taxing distributions occur in the future. But there are no immediate tax expenditures for back-loaded savings plans because only after-tax income is contributed to the account. The costs to the government are reflected in the budget only when the monies are distributed from the account. Over the long-term, a frontloaded plan may be less costly to the government than a back-loaded plan, but within the typical 5- or 10-year budget window, the back-loaded plan will look less expensive.

The tax expenditures of these tax incentives are not trivial. **Table 2** reports the estimated tax expenditures for the exclusion of contributions and earnings for employer pension plans such as 401(k) plans, IRAs, and Keogh plans, in addition to the Saver's Credit which is discussed below. The Joint Committee on Taxation estimates that the FY2007 retirement income related tax expenditures will amount to $133.8 billion, which is equivalent to 84.7% of the Congressional Budget Office's estimate of the FY2007 federal budget deficit. By FY2011, these tax expenditures are estimated to reach $175.7 billion.

Table 2. Estimates of Tax Expenditures, 2007-2011 (Billions of Dollars)

	Fiscal Year				
	2007	**2008**	**2009**	**2010**	**2011**
Employer Plans	$108.6	$114.1	$120.4	$126.7	$137.5
IRAs	15.5	17.0	18.5	20.0	23.2
Keogh Plans	8.8	9.5	10.6	11.5	14.1
Saver's Credit	0.9	0.9	0.9	0.9	0.9
Total	**133.8**	**141.5**	**150.4**	**159.1**	**175.7**

Source: U.S. Congress, Joint Committee on Taxation, *Estimates of Federal Tax Expenditures For Fiscal Years 2007-2011*, committee print, 110th Congress, 1st sess., Sept. 24, 2007 (Washington: GPO 2007).

Furthermore, conventional economic theory and empirical analysis do not offer unambiguous evidence that these tax incentives have increased personal saving. From a theoretical perspective, the effect of a tax reduction on personal saving is ambiguous because of offsetting income and substitution effects. The increased rate of return may cause individuals to substitute future consumption for current consumption and save more (a substitution effect), but, at the same time, the higher rate of return allows individuals to save less and still obtain their target amount of savings (an income effect). The overall consequences for personal savings depends on the relative magnitude of these two effects. In the case of IRAs, personal savings may be unaffected because most of the tax benefits are provided to individuals contributing the maximum amount, which eliminates any substitution effect. Casual observation suggests that the income effect dominates since the personal saving rate has fallen since the introduction of IRAs and 401(k) plans. The empirical evidence on the relationship of tax incentives to the saving rate mostly comes from examinations of traditional IRAs and 401(k) plans. The reported results are mixed, but generally indicate small effects.[27] Furthermore, Roth IRAs eliminate the immediate reward to retirement saving because the contributions are not tax deductible and may thus reduce saving.

In general, many tax incentives to increase saving tend to benefit higher-income individuals and families to a much greater extent than lower-income individuals and families. The primary reasons are (1) higher-income individuals are much more likely to save, and (2) higher-income individuals face higher marginal tax rates and benefit more from sheltering income from taxation. Furthermore, with regards to educational savings plans, the penalties for using the educational savings for noneducational purposes may discourage lower-income families from having these accounts. Children from lower-income families are less likely to attend college than other children, thus increasing the likelihood of being penalized for having an education savings account. These penalties partly explain why parents participating in Coverdell Education Savings Accounts (ESAs) and 529 plans have substantially higher income, on average, than other parents.[28]

The Economic Growth and Tax Relief Reconciliation Act of 2001 (P.L. 107-16) provided low- and moderate-income individuals a nonrefundable tax credit for contributions to a qualified retirement plan (the Saver's Credit).[29] The maximum amount of the tax credit is $2,000. The savings effects of this tax credit have not been fully evaluated yet, but early evidence suggests that many taxpayers are unable to receive the full benefit because the credit is nonrefundable.[30] In addition, the Saver's Credit appears to be substantially less effective in boosting saving among low-income individuals than a simple matching contribution possibly because of the complexity of the Saver's Credit and the tax system in general.[31]

Other Inducements

There are at least four other inducements that have been used to encourage savings for specific purposes. First, an initial or supplemental contribution can be placed in an individual's savings account. An example is the 1% agency contribution placed in a federal employee's Thrift Savings Plan (TSP) account.[32] This contribution is placed in the account whether or not the employee chooses to make contributions to his or her account. This can encourage individuals to save by overcoming the inertia to open an account, and it allows individuals to observe the benefits of saving (for example, interest compounding) without risking their own money. Once the benefits of saving are experienced, individuals may be more willing to commit their own funds to the savings account.

Second, matching contributions can be made to an individual's account. This is a common practice in many 401(k) pension plans, including the federal Thrift Saving Plan. In the case of 401(k) pensions, part or all of an employee's contribution is matched by the employer. The more the employee contributes, the more the employer contributes up to a limit. The employer is essentially supplementing the employee's salary, but only if the employee saves. Empirical evidence suggests that small matching contributions (about 10 cents for every dollar saved) will increase employees' contributions. But increasing matching contributions past this point may have no effect on an employee's contributions or actually reduce his or her contributions.[33] If an employee has a set target for saving, for example, then increasing the employer's contribution means that the employee can save less and still meet his or her saving target. Limited evidence suggests that matching contributions could significantly increase contributions by low- and moderate-income families.[34]

Third, tax-favored savings initially could be used only for a specific purpose, such as retirement in the case of 401(k) plans, and individuals faced a penalty for nonqualified uses of the savings. The penalty helps commit individuals to hold the funds for the desired purpose (such as retirement) rather than use them for current consumption. But individuals may be reluctant to give up the freedom to use the funds for other equally important purposes as individuals try to balance saving for retirement and saving for precautionary reasons. Over time, however, laws and regulations were changed to allow employees to borrow from their 401(k) plan or to make penalty-free withdrawals for emergency purposes. In addition to retirement after age 59½, qualified (that is, penalty-free) distributions can be made from IRAs for educational expenses, first-time home purchase, and medical expenses. There is some empirical evidence that pre-retirement access to 401(k) funds increases participation in and contributions to 401(k) pension plans.[35] But allowing preretirement access to 401(k) assets could also lead some to have smaller pension balances at retirement if the borrowed funds are never repaid or if withdrawn funds are never replaced.

Fourth, some firms have experimented with changing the default options for pension plans where participation is voluntary. For example, employees are covered by a firm's 401(k) plan only if they actively sign up and enroll in the plan. However, through inertia many employees do not participate. The default option, therefore, combines with worker inertia to yield low saving rates and little retirement savings. Changing the default to automatic enrollment means the employee has to actively opt out of the pension plan.[36] Recent evaluations of some firms that have changed to automatic enrollment shows that participation is significantly increased though this simple change. But through inertia, a substantial fraction of the new participants accept the firm's default contribution level and investment options for their pension assets.[37]

PROPOSALS TO INCREASE SAVING

In the FY2008 budget proposal, the Bush Administration proposed to encourage saving by expanding tax-free saving opportunities. The Administration proposed creating lifetime savings accounts (LSAs) and Retirement Savings Accounts (RSAs). The annual nondeductible contribution limits would be $2,000 for LSAs and $5,000 for RSAs, regardless of age or income. The RSA contribution, however, cannot be greater than earnings. The LSA and RSA would be similar to Roth IRAs in that investment earnings accumulate tax-free. Funds from the LSA could be withdrawn penalty-free at any time for any purpose, while RSA distributions would not be taxed or penalized if made after age 58, death, or disability. The annual contribution limit would be indexed to inflation.

The recent President's Advisory Panel on Federal Tax Reform proposed the creation of Save for Family Accounts (SFAs) to replace existing education and medical savings accounts, and Save for Retirement Accounts (SRAs) to replace traditional and Roth IRAs. This proposal would allow every taxpayer to contribute up to $10,000 every year to an SFA and an SRA on an after-tax basis.[38] The earnings would accumulate tax-free in the same way as in the current Roth IRA. Tax-free withdrawals would be allowed at any time from the SFA for qualified educational and medical costs, or to purchase a primary residence. In addition, taxpayers would be able to withdraw up to $1,000 tax-free each year for any purpose. Nonqualified distributions in excess of the $1,000 limit would be subject to income taxes and a 10% penalty tax, similar to the penalty paid on nonqualified distributions from the current Roth IRA. Tax-free withdrawals from SRAs would be allowed after age 58, death, or disability. Nonqualified withdrawals would be subject to the income tax and a 10% penalty tax.

Both the Bush Administration proposal and the President's Advisory Panel plan shift savings incentives from the front-loaded form to the back-loaded form. Most of the arguments regarding increasing private saving, however, apply to front-loaded savings plans. Back-loaded plans or Roth IRAs eliminate (1) the immediate reward to retirement saving (the tax deduction), and (2) the need to save for future tax liabilities. Consequently, shifting from front-loaded to back-loaded savings approaches may reduce personal savings. In addition, the long-term revenue loss from these proposals could be substantial thus leading to a large reduction in public saving.[39] The result of these savings proposals could be a large reduction in national saving and a reduction in economic growth.

The Administration also proposed the establishment of Individual Development Accounts (IDAs) for lower-income individuals and families. Eligible individuals and families could set up IDAs with qualified entities who would then match the first $500 contributed in a taxable year.[40] Contributions would not be tax deductible and investment earnings would be subject to tax, but the matching contributions and associated investment earnings would be tax-free. Qualified withdrawals could be made from IDAs for higher education, first-time home purchase, business start-up, or qualified rollovers. Withdrawals for other purposes could result in forfeiture of some or all of the matching contributions and earnings. IDAs could increase personal saving by stimulating new saving by low- and moderate-income taxpayers. The matching contributions would reduce public saving but increase personal savings by the same amount. The overall effect on national saving would, therefore, likely be positive.

A recent proposal offered by analysts at the Brookings Institution moves away from reliance on tax incentives to encourage retirement saving.[41] The proposal has several elements designed to remove behavioral barriers to saving. The two major elements are (1) automatic enrollment in 401(k) plans or in an IRA if the employer does not sponsor a pension plan, and (2) a 30% government matching contribution. The government contribution would replace the current tax deduction for retirement saving contributions. Other elements include allowing participants to borrow from their retirement account, and removing retirement savings from the asset test for public assistance eligibility.

CONCLUSIONS

Various motives have been identified as to why people save, and survey evidence suggests that people know why they should save. However, many people do not save. Many reasons have been offered to explain low saving rates and low savings. Economic barriers to saving include disincentives induced by government policies and life-cycle changes in the propensity to save. Behavioral explanations for low savings stress that individuals can make choices that are unfavorable to themselves. To overcome these barriers, the government offers a variety of saving incentives.

Most of the government incentives to save come through the tax system. For FY2007, these tax incentives are estimated to cost the U.S. Treasury $133.8 billion in forgone tax revenues — almost 85% of the estimated FY2007 budget deficit. The tax incentives primarily benefit higher-income families because they (1) are more likely to save, and (2) face higher marginal tax rates and thus benefit more from sheltering income from taxation. The tax incentives, however, appear to be relatively ineffective in inducing new saving — many of the families benefitting from the tax incentives likely shifted funds from other saving accounts into the tax-preferred accounts. Consequently, public saving is lower because of the forgone tax revenues due to the tax incentives while personal saving may be only slightly increased at best. In designing pro-saving policies, it is important to consider the aggregate effects of the policies on all components of national savings, both public and private.

The Bush Administration and the President's Advisory Panel on Federal Tax Reform have advocated expanding tax incentives as the primary policy to encourage saving. Personal saving has been shown to be fairly unresponsive to tax incentives, however, and they may substantially decrease public saving (that is, increase the budget deficit). The long-term net effect on national saving is likely negative. Other proposals offered by retirement experts are designed to (1) overcome behavioral barriers to saving, and (2) redistribute the benefits of government saving incentives more broadly across the population. These proposals could increase personal saving, but could also decrease public saving.

End Notes

[1] The term saving refers to the flow of resources not consumed and represents additions to wealth. Savings is a synonym for wealth.

[2] See CRS Report RL30873, *Saving in the United States: How Has It Changed and Why Is It Important?* by Brian W. Cashell and Gail Makinen.

[3] See Asena Caner and Edward N. Wolff, "Asset Poverty in the United States, 1984-1999: Evidence from the Panel Study of Income Dynamics," *Review of Income and Wealth*, vol. 50, no. 4 (Dec. 2004), pp. 493-518. The authors adopt the definition of "asset poor" as a household whose "access to 'wealth-type resources' is insufficient to enable the household to meet its 'basic needs' for some limited 'period of time.'" They choose the poverty threshold as their definition of basic needs and three months as the limited period of time.

[4] See, for example, B. Douglas Bernheim and John Karl Scholz, "Private Saving and Public Policy," in James M. Poterba, ed., *Tax Policy and the Economy, Vol. 7* (Cambridge, MA: MIT Press, 1993), pp. 73-110; and Alicia H. Munnell, Anthony Webb, and Luke Delorme, *A New National Retirement Risk Index*, Center for Retirement Research at Boston College, Issue Brief no. 48, Jun. 2006.

[5] See, for example, Edward Gramlich, "The Importance of Raising National Saving," speech at the Benjamin Rush Lecture, Dickinson College, PA, Mar. 2, 2005.

[6] Only Iceland and Portugal have lower national saving rates than the United States. See *OECD in Figures*, OECD Observer 2006, Supplement 1.

[7] The figure shows net saving rather than gross saving. Gross saving includes depreciation allowances destined to replace existing capital. Net saving represents resources from forgoing consumption that are available to increase the stock of capital.

[8] See David W. Wilcox, "Household Spending and Saving: Measurement, Trends, and Analysis," *Federal Reserve Bulletin*, vol. 77, no. 1 (Jan. 1991), pp. 1-17.

[9] John Maynard Keynes, *The General Theory of Employment, Interest and Money* (London: MacMillan and Co., 1936), pp. 107-108.

[10] See Martin Browning and Annamaria Lusardi, "Household Saving: Micro Theories and Micro Facts," *Journal of Economic Literature*, vol. 34, no. 4 (Dec. 1996), pp. 1797-1855. As an example, qualifying for a mortgage with no private mortgage insurance requires a down payment of 20%.

[11] Families are divided into the top half or the bottom half of the income distribution based on total family income.

[12] See Alan J. Auerbach and Laurence J. Kotlikoff, "Demographics, Fiscal Policy, and U.S. Saving in the 1980s and Beyond," in Lawrence H. Summers, ed., *Tax Policy and the Economy, Vol. 4* (Cambridge, MA: MIT Press, 1990), pp. 73-101.

[13] See Alan J. Auerbach, Laurence J. Kotlikoff, and David N. Weil, *The Increasing Annuitization of the Elderly — Estimates and Implications for Intergenerational Transfers, Inequality, and National Saving*, National Bureau of Economic Research, Working Paper no. 4182, Oct. 1992.

[14] See Lawrence Summers and Chris Carrol, "Why Is U.S. National Saving So Low?" Brookings Institution, *Brookings Papers on Economic Activity*, no. 1, 1987, pp. 607-635.

[15] See Erik Hurst, Annamaria Lusardi, Arthur Kennickell, and Francisco Torralba, *Precautionary Savings and the Importance of Business Owners*, National Bureau of Economic Research, Working Paper no. 11731, Nov. 2005.

[16] R. Glenn Hubbard, Jonathan Skinner, and Stephen P. Zeldes, "Precautionary Saving and Social Insurance," *Journal of Political Economy*, vol. 103, no. 2 (1995), p. 393.

[17] Society of Actuaries, *2005 Risks and Process of Retirement Survey: Report of Findings*, Mar. 2006, p. 5.

[18] Chris O'Brien, Paul Fenn, and Stephen Diacon, *How Long Do People Expect to Live? Results and Implications*, Centre for Risk and Insurance Studies, Research Report 2005-1, June 2005.

[19] See, for example, Paul Courant, Edward Gramlich, and John Laitner, "A Dynamic Micro Estimate of the Life Cycle Model," in Henry J. Aaron and Gary Burtless, eds., *Retirement and Economic Behavior* (Washington, DC: Brookings Institution, 1986); and B. Douglas Bernheim, Jonathan Skinner, and Steven Weinberg, "What Accounts for the Variation in Retirement Wealth Among U.S. Households?" *American Economic Review*, vol. 91, no. 4 (Sept. 2001.), pp. 832-857.

[20] Brigitte C. Madrian and Dennis F. Shea, "The Power of Suggestion: Inertia in 401(k) Participation and Savings Behavior," *Quarterly Journal of Economics*, vol. 116, no. 4 (Nov. 2001), pp. 1149-1187.

[21] See, for example, Richard H. Thaler, "Psychology and Savings Policies," *American Economic Review*, vol. 84, no. 2 (May 1994), pp. 186-192.

[22] Amar Cheema and Dilip Soman, "Malleable Mental Accounting: The Effect of Flexibility on the Justification of Attractive Spending and Consumption Decisions," *Journal of Consumer Psychology*, vol. 16, no. 1 (2006), pp. 33-44.

[23] See, for example, Herbert A. Simon, *The Sciences of the Artificial, 2nd Edition* (Cambridge, MA: MIT Press, 1981).

[24] Annamaria Lusardi, "Information, Expectations, and Savings for Retirement," in Henry J. Aaron, ed., *Behavioral Dimensions of Retirement Economics* (Washington, DC: Brookings Institution, 1999).

[25] For a discussion of many of the issues with regards to IRAs see CRS Report RL30255, *Individual Retirement Accounts (IRAs): Issues and Proposed Expansion*, by Thomas L. Hungerford and Jane G. Gravelle.

[26] The cost of tax incentives are measured in terms of tax expenditures, which are estimates of the revenue losses attributable to provisions of federal tax laws.

[27] For a more complete discussion of the savings literature, see Jane G. Gravelle, *The Economic Effects of Taxing Capital Income* (Cambridge, MA: MIT Press, 1994), p. 27 for a discussion of the general empirical literature on savings and pp. 193-197 for a discussion of the empirical studies of IRAs. Subsequent to this survey, a paper by Orazio P. Attanasio and Thomas C. DeLeire, "The Effect of Individual Retirement Accounts on Household Consumption and National Savings," *Economic Journal*, vol. 112 (July 2002), pp. 504-538 found little evidence that IRAs increased savings. For additional surveys see the three articles published in the *Journal of Economic Perspectives*, vol. 10, no. 3 (Fall 1996): R. Glenn Hubbard and Jonathan Skinner, "Assessing the Effectiveness of Savings Incentives," (pp. 73-90); James M. Poterba, Steven F. Venti and David A. Wise, "How Retirement Savings Programs Increase Saving," (pp. 91-113); Eric M. Engen, William G. Gale, and John Karl Scholz, "The Illusory Effects of Savings Incentives on Saving," (pp. 113-138). A working paper by Alun Thomas and Christopher Towe, "U.S. Private Saving and the Tax Treatment of IRA/401(k)s: A Re-examination Using Household Saving Data," International Monetary Fund working paper 96/87 Aug. 1996 found that IRAs did not increase private household saving. A more recent study by Eric M. Engen and William G. Gale found that 401(k) plans, which are similar to IRAs in important ways, had a negligible to modest effect on savings. See "The Effects of 401(k) Plans on Household Wealth: Differences Across Earnings Groups," National Bureau for Economic Research working paper 8032, Dec. 2000. See also Douglas H. Joines and James G. Manegold, "IRAs and Savings: Evidence from a Panel of Taxpayers," Federal Reserve Bank of Kansas City research working paper 91-05, Oct. 1991; Daniel J. Benjamin, "Does 401(k) Eligibility Increase Saving? Evidence from Propensity Score Subclassification," Journal of Public Economics, vol. 83, no. 5-6 (2003), pp. 1259-1290; and Orazio P. Attanasio, James Banks, and Matthew Wakefield, "Effectiveness of Tax Incentives to Boost (Retirement) Savings: Theoretical Motivation and Empirical Evidence," *OECD Economic Studies* No. 39, 2004/2, pp. 145-172, which all present evidence that retirement saving tax incentives induce very little new saving.

[28] See Susan Dynarski, "Who Benefits from the Education Saving Incentives? Income, Educational Expectations and the Value of the 529 and Coverdell," *National Tax Journal*, vol. 57, no. 2 (June 2004), pp. 359-383; Sarah Holden, "Saving for College with 529 Plans," paper presented the Ninety-fifth Annual Conference on Taxation, Orlando, FL, Nov. 16, 2002; and Jennifer Ma, *Education Saving Incentives and Household Saving: Evidence from the 2000 TIAA-CREF Survey of Participants*, National Bureau of Economic Research Working Paper no. 9505, Feb. 2003.

[29] For a description of the Saver's Credit see William G. Gale, J. Mark Iwry, and Peter Orszag, *The Saver's Credit: Expanding Retirement Savings for Middle- and Lower-Income Americans*, The Retirement Security Project, Issue Brief no. 2005-2, Mar. 2005.

[30] See Gary Koenig and Robert Harvey, "Utilization of the Saver's Credit: An Analysis of the First Year," *National Tax Journal*, vol. 58, no. 4 (Dec. 2005), pp. 787-806.

[31] See Ester Duflo, William Gale, Jeffrey Liebman, Peter Orszag, and Emmanuel Saez, *Saving Incentives for Low- and Middle-Income Families: Evidence from a Field Experiment with H&R Block*, National Bureau of Economic Research, Working Paper no. 11680, Sept. 2005.

[32] This applies only to federal employees in the Federal Employee Retirement System (FERS) system and not to employees in the Civil Service Retirement System (CSRS).

[33] See Leslie E. Papke, "Participation in and Contributions to 401(k) Pension Plans: Evidence from Plan Data," *Journal of Human Resources*, vol. 30, no. 2 (Spring 1995), pp. 311-325.

[34] See Ester Duflo, William Gale, Jeffrey Liebman, Peter Orszag, and Emmanuel Saez, *Saving Incentives for Low- and Middle-Income Families: Evidence from a Field Experiment with H&R Block*, National Bureau of Economic Research, Working Paper no. 11680, Sept. 2005.

[35] U.S. Government Accountability Office, *401(k) Pension Plans: Loan Provisions Enhance Participation But May Affect Income Security for Some*, GAO/HEHS-98-5, Oct. 1997.

[36] For a review of IRS rulings regarding automatic enrollment in 401(k) plans, see CRS Report RS21954, *Automatic Enrollment in Section 401(k) Plans*, by Patrick Purcell.

[37] See Brigitte C. Madrian and Dennis F. Shea, "The Power of Suggestion: Inertia in 401(k) Participation and Savings Behavior," *Quarterly Journal of Economics*, vol. 116, no. 4 (Nov. 2001), pp. 1149-1187.

[38] Contributions to the SRA can not exceed earnings.

[39] See CRS Report RL32228, *Proposed Savings Accounts: Economic and Budgetary Effects*, by Jane G. Gravelle and Maxim Shvedov. The report suggests that the 10-year cost after 2015 of the Administration's proposal could be in the neighborhood of $300 to $500 billion.

[40] Eligibility is limited to U.S. citizens and legal residents between the ages of 18 and 60 years who cannot be claimed as a dependent on another taxpayer's return, with modified adjusted gross income less than $20,000 for individuals, $30,000 for heads of household, and $40,000 for married taxpayers filing a joint return.

[41] See William G. Gale, Jonathan Gruber, and Peter R. Orszag, *Improving Opportunities and Incentives for Saving by Middle- and Low-Income Households, Brookings Institution*, Hamilton Project White Paper no. 2006-02, Apr. 2006.

In: Savings in the U.S.: Effects, Issues ... ISBN: 978-1-60741-357-8
Editor: Lyman T. Randolph

Chapter 5

SAVING RATES IN THE UNITED STATES: CALCULATION AND COMPARISON

Brian W. Cashell

SUMMARY

The amount of money saved has important economic consequences. Nationally, the amount of saving determines how much can be invested and ultimately the size of the capital stock. Increasing the size of the capital stock is believed to be one way to raise the productivity of the labor force. Individually, saving is critical to accumulating sufficient wealth to maintain living standards after retirement. This report explains how national saving is measured, presents recent estimates of saving rates in the United States, and, for comparison, provides those of other major industrial countries. This report will be updated periodically.

INTRODUCTION

Anyone with income and a future must decide how much to spend and how much to save. Individuals may save a fraction of their income for precautionary reasons, as well as to provide for themselves in retirement. Businesses retain a fraction of their profits in order to finance new investments. Governments save (or dis-save) as a consequence of policy decisions about how much to tax and how much to spend.

The amount of money saved as a nation has important economic consequences. If individuals save too little during their working lives to avoid falling living standards in old age, that may influence policymakers' views about the appropriate level of Social Security taxes and benefits. National saving, the sum of individual, business, and public saving, has important consequences for the balance of trade, economic growth, and future standards of living.[1]

Although economic theory gives no reason to prefer one saving rate to another, it may still be useful to examine trends in saving and to compare U.S. saving rates with those in other countries. This report provides a brief explanation of how saving is measured, and it provides current data on saving rates in the United States and for selected foreign countries.

MEASURING SAVING

Saving, in a nutshell, is income minus consumption. In an economic sense, however, consumption is not the same as expenditures. Translating the theoretical notion of saving into a statistical measure is a challenge.

The source for U.S. saving data is the national income and product accounts (NIPA) published by the Department of Commerce, Bureau of Economic Analysis (BEA). The NIPA constitute the accounting framework which is used to produce estimates of gross domestic product (GDP). GDP is the total value of goods and services produced, and it can be calculated in two different ways. One way is to add up the value of all the goods and services produced (the product side of the accounts), and the other way is to add up all of the income earned in the production of those goods and services (the income side of the account).

On the product side, GDP is the total value of those goods and services produced for personal consumption (C), investment (I), government (G), as well as for export (X). On the income side, the income earned in the production of those goods and services can be accounted for as consumer spending (C), taxes (T), private saving (S), and spending for imported goods and services (M).

Since each of these approaches measure the same variable (GDP), they can be set equal to each other, in this way:

$$C + I + G + X = C + T + S + M$$

Subtracting consumption (C) from both sides simplifies the equality:

$$I + G + X = T + S + M$$

This can now be rearranged by subtracting government spending (G) and exports (X) from both sides, which gives:

$$I = S + (T - G) + (M - X)$$

This equation illustrates the importance of saving. Total investment is equal to the sum of private saving (S), public saving (T-G), and the net inflow of capital from abroad (MX).[2]

GROSS AND NET SAVING

In the broadest sense, saving is income less consumption. Consumption is typically taken to mean spending on goods and services by households. But consumption can also refer to the wear and tear (depreciation, or capital consumption) on the capital stock that occurs in the production of those goods and services. Thus, some saving must be allocated to the replacement of the existing capital stock as it wears out. Only if saving is more than sufficient to replace the existing capital stock as it wears out can the capital stock grow.

For this reason, saving data distinguish between "gross" and "net" saving. The difference between the two measures is the estimated deterioration in the existing capital stock. In some cases, such as computers, capital may be completely depreciated in a very short period of time, whereas in others, such as buildings or heavy equipment, capital may take a long time to wear out.

SAVING AND ECONOMIC GROWTH

Economic growth, in the long run, is determined by three factors: the growth rate of the labor force; the rate of technological progress; and the rate of growth of the capital stock.

Table 1. Accounting for Saving in the United States
(all figures as a percentage of gross domestic product)

	1997	**1998**	**1999**	**2000**	**2001**	**2002**	**2003**	**2004**	**2005**	**2006**	**2007**
Gross Personal saving	2.6	3.2	1.7	1.7	1.3	1.8	1.6	1.6	0.3	0.5	0.4
Gross Business saving	13.1	12.0	12.6	11.9	12.5	13.1	13.2	13.6	14.6	14.1	13.3
Private Capital Consumption	9.6	9.7	9.9	10.1	10.6	10.3	10.2	10.3	10.9	10.3	10.4
Gross Private Saving	15.7	15.2	14.3	13.6	13.8	14.9	14.8	15.2	14.9	14.6	13.7
Net Private Saving	6.1	5.5	4.5	3.5	3.2	4.6	4.6	4.8	3.9	4.3	3.3
Gross Federal Saving	0.3	1.4	2.0	2.8	1.3	-1.5	-2.6	-2.4	-1.6	-0.7	-0.9
Federal Capital Consumption	1.0	0.9	0.9	0.9	0.9	0.8	0.8	0.8	0.8	0.8	0.8
Net Federal Saving	**-0.7**	**0.4**	**1.1**	**1.9**	**0.5**	**-2.4**	**-3.4**	**-3.2**	**-2.3**	**-1.5**	**-1.7**
Gross S&L Government Saving	1.6	1.7	1.6	1.6	1.2	0.8	1.0	1.2	1.5	1.6	1.4
S&L Capital Consumption	1.1	1.1	1.1	1.1	1.2	1.2	1.2	1.2	1.2	1.2	1.3
Net S&L Saving	0.5	0.6	0.5	0.5	0.0	-0.3	-0.2	0.0	0.2	0.4	0.1
Gross Public Saving	1.9	3.1	3.7	4.4	2.5	-0.7	-1.6	-1.2	-0.1	0.9	0.5
Net Public Saving	**-0.2**	**1.0**	**1.7**	**2.4**	**0.5**	**-2.7**	**-3.6**	**-3.2**	**-2.1**	**-1.2**	**-1.6**
Gross National Saving	17.6	18.3	18.1	18.0	16.4	14.2	13.3	13.8	14.8	15.5	14.2
Net National Saving	5.9	6.5	6.2	5.9	3.7	1.9	1.1	1.6	1.9	3.1	1.7
Net Foreign Investment	1.3	2.1	3.0	4.0	3.7	4.4	4.7	5.3	5.7	5.9	5.2
Total Gross Domestic Investment	18.9	20.4	21.0	22.1	20.0	18.6	18.0	19.2	20.6	21.3	19.4

Source: Department of Commerce, Bureau of Economic Analysis.

The productivity of the labor force depends on both the level of technology and the size of the capital stock. The more capital there is, the more productive the labor force can be. The size of the capital stock, in turn, depends on the rate of investment.

Investment must equal saving. The amount that can be invested depends on the amount of saving. Saving more can lead to increased investment, resulting in a larger stock of capital and higher levels of productivity. Consuming less now enables more consumption in the future.

Thrift is considered by many to be a virtue, but economic theory gives no reason to prefer one saving rate over another. The amount saved is seen simply as a reflection of the trade off made between a desire to consume now and a willingness to consume less than one's current income to provide resources for the future.

HISTORICAL SAVING DATA

Table 1 presents historical estimates of U.S. saving rates since 1997. The data in the top third of the chart relate to the contribution of the private sector (personal or household saving, and business saving) to national saving, followed by data indicating the saving of the public sector, with separate accounting for the federal and state and local government. The bottom third of the table shows both total gross and net national saving, the amount of saving imported from abroad, and total investment as a percentage of gross domestic product.

INTERNATIONAL COMPARISONS

Although no particular saving rate is prescribed by economic theory, the case for saving more is sometimes argued on the grounds that either less is saved now than in prior years, or that the current saving rate is below that of other countries. **Table 2** presents data showing how national saving in the United States compares with that in other major industrial countries. These data differ somewhat from those presented in **Table 1** because the Organization for Economic Co-operation and Development (OECD) uses a different set of economic accounting rules, and because the OECD data are not revised on the same schedule as the NIPA data.

Table 2. Gross National Saving for Selected Countries (as a percentage of gross domestic product)

	United States	Canada	France	Germany	Italy	Japan	United Kingdom
1996	16.1	18.8	18.7	20.5	22.2	29.7	16.3
1997	17.3	19.6	19.9	20.7	22.2	29.8	17.4
1998	18.0	19.1	21.0	20.9	21.6	28.8	18.3
1999	17.8	20.7	21.8	20.3	21.1	27.2	16.0
2000	17.7	23.6	21.6	20.2	20.6	27.5	15.4
2001	16.1	22.2	21.3	19.5	20.9	25.8	15.6
2002	13.9	21.2	19.8	19.4	20.8	25.2	15.8
2003	12.9	21.4	19.1	19.5	19.8	25.4	15.7
2004	13.4	22.8	19.0	21.5	20.3	25.8	15.9
2005	13.5	23.7	18.5	21.8	19.6	26.8	15.1
2006	13.7	24.3	19.1	23.0	19.6	26.6	14.9

Source: Organization for Economic Co-operation and Development.

Over the period shown, Japan saved at a higher rate than any of the other countries, although its saving rate has been falling. The United Kingdom and the U.S. saving rates were the lowest of these seven countries.

Table 3. Household Saving for Selected Countries (as a percentage of gross domestic product)

	United States	Canada	France	Germany	Italy	Japan	United Kingdom[a]
1996	4.0	7.0	11.9	10.5	17.9	10.6	9.4
1997	3.6	4.9	12.8	10.1	15.1	10.3	9.5
1998	4.3	4.9	12.4	10.1	11.4	11.3	7.0
1999	2.4	4.0	12.1	9.5	10.4	10.0	5.3
2000	2.3	4.7	12.0	9.2	8.5	8.6	5.1
2001	1.8	5.2	12.7	9.4	10.5	5.0	6.4
2002	2.4	3.5	13.8	9.9	11.4	4.9	5.0
2003	2.1	2.6	12.7	10.3	10.4	3.9	4.9
2004	2.1	2.9	12.6	10.4	10.4	3.5	3.7
2005	0.5	1.6	11.8	10.5	10.0	3.9	5.6
2006	0.4	2.3	11.9	10.5	8.7	3.3	4.8
2007	0.4	1.5	12.7	10.9	6.8	3.1	2.9

Source: Organization for Economic Co-operation and Development.

a. The United Kingdom reports gross saving, the others are net saving rates.

Table 3 presents data comparing historical household saving rates for the same countries. The OECD household saving data are based on the most recent internationally comparable data.

End Notes

[1] For a discussion of public policy and saving, see CRS Report RL32119, *Can Public Policy Raise the Saving Rate?*, by Brian W. Cashell.

[2] Just as there is a balance between the income and product sides of the NIPA, there is a balance in international payments. If Americans buy more goods and services from abroad than they export, then (at least in this simplified example) the net outflow of dollars will be used by foreigners to buy dollar-denominated assets, which thus helps to finance domestic investment.

In: Savings in the U.S.: Effects, Issues and... ISBN: 978-1-60741-357-8
Editor: Lyman T. Randolph

Chapter 6

Proposed Savings Accounts: Economic and Budgetary Effects

Jane G. Gravelle[1] and Maxim Shvedov[2]

Summary

In various budget proposals, the President proposed to substitute for the current system of tax-favored individual retirement accounts (IRAs) two new accounts: lifetime savings accounts (LSAs) and retirement savings accounts (RSAs). Senator Craig Thomas of the Finance Committee and Representative Sam Johnson of the Ways and Means Committee have introduced identical bills (S. 545/H.R. 1163 and S. 546/H.R. 1162) to create LSAs and RSAs. Expanded savings accounts also were a part of the final recommendations of the President's Advisory Panel on Federal Tax Reform.

These proposals differ from the current system of IRAs in several important ways, including the required use of a back-loaded method now used for Roth but not traditional IRAs (in back-loaded accounts contributions are not deductible but withdrawals are not taxable), higher contribution limits in some cases, introduction of LSAs with no penalties for withdrawal, and elimination of income phaseouts.

Shifting to a mandatory back-loaded method, including the ability to roll over current deductible IRAs into the new system, along with some other features, has important consequences for the path of revenue loss. The Treasury projects the plans to either raise revenue or have little revenue effect in the first 10 years. CRS projections of long-run revenue costs (in the steady state beyond 2015) suggest a 10- year loss in the neighborhood of $300 to $500 billion. While it is difficult to estimate the cost precisely, the large limits and lack of strings attached suggest that a very large fraction of interest, dividends, and capital gains could be tax exempt.

Neither theory nor empirical evidence seems to present much of a case for a significant (or even positive) effect on private savings resulting from these provisions — particularly the back-loaded form. The change would tend to redistribute aftertax income on both a relative and absolute basis from lower- to higher-income groups in part because lower- and moderate-income individuals tend to have little or no savings — although benefits to the highest-income individuals would be constrained by the contributions limit.

The provision of tax favored savings accounts with high limits could have some consequences for certain activities and sectors of the economy. It could reduce the fraction of small businesses with pension plans, as owners elect to save in their private accounts rather than through accounts set up in their businesses. The provisions would also make a variety of currently favored investments less attractive, including tax exempt state and local bonds, life insurance products such as deferred annuities, and direct investments in owner-occupied housing. Some of these effects should increase economic efficiency. The change would discourage equity investment in unincorporated businesses and rental housing and favor investment in debt. It would have uncertain effects on the most heavily taxed investment, corporate equity. This report will not be updated.

In several recent budget proposals, the President proposed to substitute for the current system of individual retirement accounts (IRAs) two new arrangements: lifetime savings accounts (LSAs) and retirement savings accounts (RSAs).[1] The contribution limit for each of the new accounts was $5,000 in FY2005 — FY2007, down from $7,500 in FY2004. In FY2008 the LSA accounts were restricted to $2,000. In 2005 Senator Craig Thomas of the Finance Committee and Representative Sam Johnson of the Ways and Means Committee introduced identical bills to create LSAs (S. 545 / H.R. 1163) and RSAs (S. 546/H.R. 1162). A year earlier the same legislators sponsored similar bills (S. 2263/H.R. 4078, and H.R. 4714). The President's Advisory Panel on Federal Tax Reform proposed similar accounts, called Save for Family and Save for Retirement accounts, with $10,000 annual limits, as a part of its final recommendations.

These proposals differ from the current system of individual retirement accounts in several important ways. First, unlike the current system, no choice is allowed between a traditional or front-loaded account (where individuals deduct contributions, pay no tax on earnings, but pay tax on withdrawals, much like a pension plan) and Roth or back-loaded accounts adopted in 1997 (where no contributions are deducted and no earnings or withdrawals are taxed, as with a tax exempt bond). The new system requires all accounts to be in the back-loaded form. While both back-loaded and front-loaded accounts effectively result in a tax rate on earnings of zero (assuming constant tax rates in the case of front-loaded accounts) the revenue paths of front-loaded and back-loaded accounts are quite different — the costs of front-loaded accounts occur much more quickly than the costs of a back-loaded account.[2] Moreover, the projected revenue effect would also reflect both the involuntary substitution of back-loaded for front-loaded accounts (because the latter would no longer be allowed) and voluntary shifts of present asset balances or contributions to employer plans with discretion, such as 401(k) plans. The form of the account also has some important implications for private savings responses.

Secondly, the limits of the new accounts are higher than current accounts, amounting to contributions of $10,000 ($5,000 for each account) for the FY2007 proposal and Advisory Panel Proposal, and $7,000 for the FY2008 proposal. Married couples filing jointly would have twice the limits. The 2004 proposals supported by Senator Thomas and Representative Johnson were $15,000 ($7,500 for each account). The contribution levels of IRAs were $2,000 before the recent tax cuts and would have reverted back to this cap after 2010, but the benefits were made permanent and the new amounts were set at $5,000.[3] These higher limits also have important economic implications.

Thirdly, the LSA account is to be allowed with no penalties for withdrawal before retirement age. This feature makes this type of account, unlike the current IRA, a virtually perfect substitute for ordinary savings — and one would expect financial institutions to quickly set up simple types of accounts that would be eligible for the tax benefit. RSAs have penalties for withdrawing before age 58 (slightly below the current 59½ age) but like current Roth IRAs have no required minimum distribution after age 70½ (as do traditional, or front-loaded, IRAs).

Finally, the proposal eliminates all income limits on the accounts; very-high-income individuals are not currently eligible for the benefit, but would become so under the proposal.

Long Run Revenue Cost

The projected revenue effects of these proposals show either a small revenue gain or a small loss. The magnitude of these effects is no more than a few billion dollars over 10 years for the budget horizon, but these intermediate-term revenue effects greatly understate the eventual cost of the program beyond the budget window. This section explores a variety of approaches to estimating the long run cost that would occur after the cost has settled into a steady state, which would probably be in the tens of billions per year, and several hundred billion over a 10-year period (within the steady state, perhaps after the second or third decade). Even though the annual contribution caps differed from proposal to proposal, the revenue loss pattern is similar in every case and many conclusions remain unaffected by the difference.

The Long Run Cost Projected from Short Run Official Estimates: an Illustration

The near term revenue effects of the FY2004 LSA/RSA proposal (with the $7,500 ceiling) as projected by either the Treasury or the Joint Committee on Taxation (JCT), were very small. The President's 2004 budget proposal showed a gain of $14.8 billion in the first five years and a gain of $2 billion in the first 10 years.[4] The JCT found a similar pattern (gains, then losses), but projected quite different numbers, with a loss of $4.9 billion in 2013, an overall gain of $12 billion in the first five years, and a loss of $5 billion over the 10-year period.[5] For the FY2007 proposals, with the lower $5,000 ceiling, both Treasury and JCT project small 10-year losses of $122 million (Treasury) to $275 million (JCT).[6]

The comparable Treasury 10-year estimates for FY2006 and FY2005 proposals were $1.5 billion and $5.6 billion gains, respectively.[7] JCT's estimates of the measures were $2.4 billion and $0.9 billion losses over the 10-year period, respectively.[8] Both sets of estimates show a similar pattern of revenue gains in the first years reversing into the losses in the remainder of the period.[9]

These near-term estimates (for the next 10 years) show positive or small negative effects for three reasons. First, for any new normally taxable savings that are now funneled into these tax free accounts, the cost rises very rapidly over time compared to most tax reductions (which tend to rise at the nominal growth rate of the economy, perhaps around 5%). For example, suppose $7,500 were put into an account in each year and the interest rate is 10%. In the first year the reduction in taxable income is $750 (10% of $7,500). In the next year, the previous year's investment is now worth $8,250 ($7,500X1.10) and adding a current investment, the total in the account is now $15,750. The second year's reduction in taxable income is $1,575, or 2.1 times the first year — a growth rate of 110%. In the third year the cost is 3.31 times the first year. Based on the model shown in the appendix which allows for contributions and withdrawals which relates each year to its eventual long-term steady state, the first year's cost (expressed in current income levels) is about 3% of the steady state cost, the fifth year's cost is about 18% and the tenth year's cost is about 41%. Overall, the first five years' cost is about 11% of a steady-state five-year cost, and the first 10 years' cost is about 20%. Thus, these losses are only a fraction of their long run losses.

Secondly, there would be a temporary revenue gain because repeal of traditional IRA provisions would reduce the cost of up-front deductions. In order to determine the loss from the expanded limits, we need to eliminate this revenue, to measure the loss, and then use the revenue pattern discussed above to project from the short term to the long term. Using this approach, we project the cost with the $7,500 limit to be at least $18 billion per year ($180 billion over 10 years with constant income levels) using the Treasury estimates. The annual cost would be slightly over $20 billion with the JCT estimates. The cost with the $5,000 limit (Treasury estimates) is about $17 billion.[10] Again, these are conservative measures.

Thirdly, individuals are allowed to roll over existing accounts into back-loaded accounts and pay for the cost over four years. Since these effects are in the first four years, we can extrapolate from a single year past that point where the cost is expected to be about 18% of the steady state. Those calculations suggest an annual cost of closer to $40 billion with relatively little difference between the $5,000 and $7,500 ceiling.[11] The projections from the Joint Tax Committee's estimates would, however, have been smaller (about $28 billion, for the $7,500 cap). These estimates would be affected by recent legislation that allows a one-time rollover of IRAs into Roth IRAs with no income limit in 2010.

Fourthly, the revenue estimates may also include some gain from the possibility of shifting some of the amounts currently contributed to 401(k) and similar plans to individual accounts (at least for amounts without an employer match), given there are no strings attached. These choices have the same types of effects as prospective future IRAs and further expand the scope for additional revenue loss.

Finally, the long run revenue cost will be slightly larger (although the effect will probably be small[12]) by the replacement of front-loaded by back-loaded accounts.

The implication from this extrapolation exercise is that the long-run steady-state revenue cost of the plans will be in the tens of billions of dollars per year, and even without accounting for all of the contributions to cost, could amount to as much $40 billion per year or $400 billion over 10 years, while the short run effect, at least according to the administration estimates, is a gain of several billion over 10 years — a dramatic contrast.

Direct Estimates of the Steady State Cost

The previous numbers extrapolated from the presumed use of these savings accounts by the Treasury and JCT revenue estimators. Another approach is to examine the total revenue collected from passive forms of investment and to estimate what fraction of that revenue will become tax exempt under the proposed plan. Since the LSA accounts have no strings attached, individuals should prefer to place all of their savings up to the limit in these accounts, including non-retirement savings. The $5,000 or $7,000 limit (and even the $2,000 limit) for each of these plans is so great that the plans could allow all savings of moderate income individuals to be contained in the account over a period of time, particularly for married couples whose LSA annual amounts would be twice as large and combined LSA and RSA amounts would be $20,000 or $30,000. Over 10 years, savings could cumulate to as much as $300,000, an amount much greater than the typical liquid savings of most families. Thus, these families would not be expected to be constrained by the limit.

In 2000, according to the Internal Revenue Service Statistics of Income (Individual returns) dividends and interest on taxable returns were $186 billion and $140 billion, respectively. There were also capital gains distributions of $61 billion, and net gain from sales of capital assets of $623 billion. The $623 billion would include non-passive investments such as real estate and would be highly concentrated among high income individuals. Just considering interest, dividends, and capital gains distributions, the total is $387 billion, which, at a 20% marginal tax rate, would yield $77 billion in revenue, implying a potential loss from the LSA/RSA plan in that vicinity (or greater, since it excludes sales of capital assets) if virtually all assets were eventually to be placed in these plans.

The actual revenue loss would be smaller than this amount for two reasons. First, the amount already excluded from individual retirement accounts under permanent rules could change because of rising income limits (although comparisons of tax expenditure projections suggest this effect is only a few billion dollars).

Table 1. Accrued Earnings on Investments of $5,000 Per Year

	Real rate of return on asset			
Years held	**3%**	**4%**	**5%**	**6%**
10	$2,915	$3,688	$4,451	$5,480
20	$6,850	$9,191	$12,027	$15,467
30	$12,163	$17,400	$36,557	$50,496
40	$19,334	$29,647	$44,723	$66,822

Source: CRS calculations; see text. The inflation rate is assumed to be 2%.

More importantly, some share of this amount is in high income brackets where a substantial portion of individuals might exceed the limit ($133 billion of the $387 billion is in the $100,000 and over income class). And even among more moderate income classes, some individuals will exceed the dollar limits.

To explore how much this revenue cost might be reduced by individuals saving more than the maximum amount, we first determine how much would be earned from accounts assuming the maximum had been saved and reinvested every year. The formulas for calculating these effects are shown in the appendix; in **Tables 1 and 2**, we show the dollar amount of earnings, depending on the real interest rate and the period of time that the asset is accumulating, for limits of $5,000 and $7,500, respectively. Note that these are the amounts accrued by a single taxpayer; a married couple would be able to save twice as much. They are also the amounts for the LSA rather than the combined IRA/LSA accounts.

Table 2. Accrued Earnings on Investments of $7,500 Per Year

	Real rate of return on asset			
Years held	**3%**	**4%**	**5%**	**6%**
10	$4,373	$5,533	$6,811	$8,221
20	$10,276	$13,787	$18,041	$23,201
30	$18,254	$26,101	$36,557	$50,496
40	$29,001	$44,471	$67,085	$100,231

Source: CRS calculations; see text. The inflation rate is assumed to be 2%.

The exact amount of exempt relevant passive income would vary for every taxpayer depending on such factors as the amount of individual annual contributions and withdrawals, years of participation in the program, and the rate of return on a person's investments. Modeling each of these parameters is not possible without detailed data, particularly data that reflect age (which is not provided on tax returns). In order to estimate the magnitude of the impact, we consider several scenarios and combine them with the historic tax return data.

Sources of the relevant passive income were limited to taxable interest, dividends, and capital gains distributions in one scenario. There are several other sources of income, in particular capital gains on sales of capital assets, and much of these gains (largely representing capital gains on stock sales) is also passive income. We provide a second scenario that includes these gains as well. The 1999 income amounts were not adjusted for inflation, although that is unlikely to have a significant influence on the results.

We ignore expansions in the regular individual retirement accounts, which would increase the maximum amount that could be sheltered in the savings plans, but whose use is more difficult to predict. Ignoring RSAs would also understate the cost, particularly keeping in mind a higher contribution limit of $5,000 under the proposal. We also ignore the offsetting effect of interest earned on checking accounts, where LSA treatment would not be feasible.

As shown in **Table 3**, three illustrative annual tax-exempt LSA income threshold values of $5,000, $15,000 and $35,000 per person are selected. Thus, married filers would effectively face caps of $10,000, $30,000, and $70,000 correspondingly. The estimation process applies these assumed thresholds to a sample of historic 1999 individual income tax returns supplied by the IRS.[13]

Table 3. Revenue Impact Under Assumed Thresholds in a Steady State

Assumed threshold value, $	Revenue impact, without sales of capital assets, $ billions	Revenue impact, with sales of capital assets, $ billions
5,000	26.7	31.4
15,000	43.2	55
35,000	54.1	75.4

Source: CRS calculations; see text.

For example, consider two single taxpayers' returns in the case of a $5,000 threshold: the first one with the sum of interest, dividends, and capital gains distributions in 1999 of $3,000 and the second one with $11,000. Under the $5,000 assumption, the first taxpayer would be able to exempt all of the relevant passive income, since it is less than $5,000. The second one would be able to exclude just the first $5,000 of $11,000, and pay the tax on the remaining $6,000. Under $15,000 or $35,000 cap scenarios, both of them would be exempt on all of their relevant passive income. Therefore, the sum of these taxpayers' deductions in the first case of $8,000 would increase to $14,000 in the second case, because of the higher income taxpayer's increased LSA deduction.

As the cap value increases, the impact grows larger, because higher income taxpayers could exempt larger shares of their relevant passive income and each dollar deducted by taxpayers in higher marginal tax brackets would be costlier than the one deducted by taxpayers in lower marginal tax rate brackets. The revenue cost increases much more slowly, proportionally, than does the cap. A tripling of the cap increases costs by 60%; a seven-fold increase doubles the cost.

The results are sensitive to the limits chosen, but even the very modest $5,000 limit indicates a cost of $27 billion per year. Since close to half of all capital gains is typically associated with sales of stock,[14] if we take the intermediate limit of $15,000 (associated with a savings period of around 25 years at a 4% to 5% return with a $5,000 limit) and average the last two columns, the estimate is around $50 billion. The general magnitude of effects is consistent with a study last year by Burman, Gale, and Orzag, who used a similar approach to estimate the FY2004 revenue loss, which they project to be in the neighborhood of $50 billion at current (2003) income levels.[15] (Given the modest increase in revenue cost with an increase in limits at this level, there is probably not a lot of difference between the $5,000 and $7,500 limit).

One revenue cost that is not included in this analysis is the loss arising from arbitrage. For example, individuals who actually have smaller savings than that eligible for IRAs could potentially borrow from a home equity line of credit and reinvest in IRAs creating an artificial tax saving. This artificial tax saving would be constrained by the spread between the rate charged on loans and the rate earned on investments, but it is possible that markets will develop to take account of such arbitrage possibilities.

Projections from Current Costs of IRAs

A final way of gaining some notion of the magnitude of long run revenue cost is to consider the tax expenditure estimate for the current IRA provision, which is $20 billion, according to thc tax expenditure compendium for 2008, the last year for which estimates have been made.[16] Some provisions have been in the law a long time, others since 1997, and the most recent changes were made in 2003 (and reflecting a limit of $5,000), so the provision is below its steady-state level. If one just recognized that the dollar limits will be tripled (in comparison to the $5,000 cap), if everyone tripled the size of the assets in their accounts, the cost would be an additional $40 billion. This estimate is overstated because all individuals will not be at the ceiling, so that one could not simply add $40 billion to account for this effect. However, the income limits will be completely removed, which would add to the cost, and the cost is not at its steady-state level. The cost would also be larger if compared to a $2,000 limit. But, in general, since current IRA provisions are relatively costly (i.e. $20 billion), it should not be surprising that such a dramatic expansion is also quite costly and could, again, easily be in the tens of billions of dollars.

Summing Up the Evidence for Long-Run Costs

While it is not possible to place a precise price tag on the long run cost of these proposals, they are clearly much more costly than is suggested by the near-term revenue estimates. An estimate of $300 to $500 billion, or even more, over a 10-year period does not seem unreasonable — a significant contrast to the $2 billion revenue gain in the short run projected by the Treasury for its FY2004 proposal, the $4 billion loss projected by the Joint Committee on Taxation for that same plan, or the $5.5 billion gain projected by the Treasury for the FY2005 proposal.[17] This huge discrepancy occurs for two reasons: the losses from additional savings in tax favored forms are small in the short run relative to the long run, and the temporary short- run revenue gains from the substitution of back-loaded for front-loaded plans and rollovers is large enough to more or less offset these losses.

ECONOMIC EFFECTS: SAVINGS, DISTRIBUTIONAL EFFECTS AND INTERACTION WITH OTHER TAX FAVORED SAVINGS

Several important economic issues arise with respect to expanding savings incentives. The focus of the Administration and perhaps of other supporters of the plan is to increase savings and economic growth. Critics are often concerned about distributional effects; savings incentives tend to favor higher income individuals. The ceilings on contributions, however, limits the benefit available to high income individuals. The expansion of tax preferred savings vehicles, particularly a general one, will have consequences for other tax favored forms including pensions, individual retirement accounts directed at pensions, tax favored educational savings accounts, and other forms of tax preferred investment income including tax exempt bonds and life insurance annuities. This section discusses these economic effects.

Effects on Savings

There has been extensive debate about the effect of individual retirement accounts on savings.[18] This debate has addressed both theoretical and empirical evidence on savings incentives in general, and on the particular effects of individual retirement accounts, which were made available to all individuals in the period 1981-1986.

If one begins with overall evidence on savings with incentives without caps or strings attached, even this evidence does not necessarily suggest private savings would increase. The effect of a tax reduction on savings is theoretically ambiguous because of offsetting income and substitution effects. The increased rate of return may cause individuals to substitute future for current consumption and save more (a substitution effect), but, at the same time, the higher rate of return will allow individuals to save less and still obtain a larger target amount (an income effect). The overall consequence for savings depends on the relative magnitude of these two effects.

Empirical evidence on the relationship of the rate of return to the saving rate is mixed, indicating mostly small effects of uncertain direction. Thus, individual contributions to IRAs may have resulted from a shifting of existing assets into IRAs or a diversion of savings that would otherwise have occurred into IRAs. A more stark illustration of the uncertainty of increasing savings with a higher rate of return is the juxtaposition of high returns in the stock market with a dramatic reduction in the personal savings rate — suggesting that income or wealth effects dominated behavior. This fall in the savings rate in the face of high returns provides some additional evidence that expanded IRAs may not be successful in increasing savings rates.

IRAs are even less likely to increase savings because they are subject to contribution limits. For those who have saving in excess of the limit, there is no marginal incentive. In this case, only the income effect dominates.

There is one caveat about this theoretical point — in the case of front-loaded (or traditional) IRAs, there is some reason to expect that the tax cut itself would be saved or largely saved. That is because the savings plan has a future tax liability attached to it (when withdrawn) so that even if an individual were not affected by the savings incentives in the normal way, he or she would wish to save the tax cut to pay the future tax. (This choice would keep consumption fixed.) This analysis applies, however, only to front-loaded IRAs, and not to the back-loaded forms in the Administration proposal.

Note that despite this conventional analysis of IRAs and savings, some economists have argued that IRA contributions were largely new savings. The theoretical argument has been made that the IRAs increase savings because of psychological, "mental account," or advertising reasons. Individuals may need the attraction of a large initial tax break; they may need to set aside funds in accounts that are restricted to discipline themselves to maintain retirement funds; or they mayneed the impetus of an advertising campaign to remind them to save.

There has also been some empirical evidence presented to suggest that IRAs increase savings. This evidence includes both some simple observations that individuals who invested in IRAs did not reduce their non-IRA assets and a variety of statistical studies, especially estimates by Venti and Wise, that showed that IRA contributions were primarily new savings.[19]

However, the fact that individuals with IRAs do not decrease their other assets does not prove that IRA contributions were new savings; it may simply mean that individuals who were planning to save in any case chose the tax-favored IRA mechanism. The Venti and Wise estimate has been criticized on theoretical grounds and another study by Gale and Scholz using similar data found no evidence of a savings effect.[20] A study by Manegold and Joines comparing savings behavior of those newly eligible for IRAs and those already eligible for IRAs found no evidence of an overall effect on savings, although increases were found for some individuals and decreases for others; a study by Attanasio and DeLeire also using this approach found little evidence of an overall savings effect.[21] And, while one must be careful in making observations from a single episode, there was no overall increase in the savings rate during the period that IRAs were universally available, despite large contributions to IRAs. Similarly, the household savings rate continued (and actually accelerated) its decline after expansion of IRAs in 1997.[22]

An important issue for evaluating the Administration proposal is that, in any case, the argument regarding private savings of the up front benefit and the debate on the psychological effects of IRAs on savings concerned the effects of front-loaded, or deductible, IRAs. These arguments do not apply to back-loaded IRAs. If the objective of the plan were to encourage private savings, the front-loaded form would have been more appropriate. Indeed, by repealing the front-loaded form and requiring back-loaded approaches, there should be a direct reduction in savings from this effect, even if savings incentives otherwise have no effect on savings. Individuals who now effectively "prepay" their taxes (which gives the government its revenue gain) should reduce their savings by an equal amount.

Of course, the effectiveness of an expansion of IRAs is also affected by contribution limits, since anyone contributing at the limit would not be affected at the margin. For some individuals, there is currently no marginal effect but would now be one which would tend to induce savings; for other new contributors who are still at the limit, there would be no marginal effect and the income effects will reduce savings. Higher contribution limits increase the fraction of revenue loss that is associated with marginal investment. Nevertheless as shown in **Tables 4 and 5**, under our simulations, a significant amount of revenue goes to individuals who are at the maximum limit (excluding sales of capital assets, 56% at the lower limit and 24% at the higher limit).

Table 4. Revenue Impact and Contributions Limits in a Steady State, Excluding Sales of Capital Assets

Assumed threshold value	Total revenue impact	Revenue impact from returns with			
		Passive income below threshold		Passive income over threshold	
$	$ million	$ million	%	$ million	%
5,000	26,698	11,802	44.2	14,896	55.8
15,000	43,106	26,576	61.7	16,530	38.3
35,000	54,150	41,424	76.5	12,726	23.5

Source: CRS calculations.

Table 5. Revenue Impact and Contribution Limits in a Steady State, Including Sales of Capital Assets

Assumed threshold value	Total revenue impact	Revenue impact from returns with			
		Passive income below threshold		Passive income over threshold	
$	$ million	$ million	%	$ million	%
5,000	31,408	16,579	52.8%	14,829	47.2%
15,000	55,020	38,399	69.8%	16,620	30.2%
35,000	75,379	62,322	82.7%	13,056	17.3%

Source: CRS calculations.

This discussion relates only to private savings. If the deficit increases in the long run, then national savings could fall even if private savings did rise.

Most of the evidence presented here suggests that the proposal is unlikely to increase savings, or if it does increase savings, the effects would be small. However, one point is clear: by choosing a form of subsidy that reduces short-run revenue costs, the Administration is also choosing a form that is least likely to increase private savings and most likely to reduce them.

Table 6. Illustrative Distributional Effects of the Proposal Under Assumed Thresholds in a Steady State, Excluding Gains on Sales of Capital Assets

Assumed threshold		$5,000			$15,000			$35,000		
AGI range ($000s)		Share of liability reduction	Average reduction per return, $	Reduction as a share of AGI	Share of liability reduction	Average reduction per return, $	Reduction as a share of AGI	Share of liability reduction	Average reduction per return, $	Reduction as a share of AGI
0	10	1.22%	12	0.40%	0.78%	12	0.41%	0.62%	12	0.41%
10	20	4.96%	54	0.36%	3.71%	65	0.44%	2.94%	65	0.44%
20	30	6.10%	87	0.35%	5.06%	116	0.47%	4.10%	119	0.48%
30	40	6.41%	127	0.37%	5.56%	178	0.51%	4.73%	192	0.55%
40	50	6.81%	179	0.40%	6.37%	269	0.60%	5.79%	309	0.69%
50	75	16.93%	263	0.43%	15.77%	394	0.65%	14.44%	457	0.75%
75	100	14.92%	500	0.58%	14.21%	766	0.89%	13.33%	909	1.06%
100	200	22.88%	846	0.64%	23.01%	1,369	1.04%	22.85%	1,720	1.30%
200	500	13.34%	1,857	0.64%	15.84%	3,547	1.23%	17.80%	5,039	1.74%
500	1000	3.88%	2,904	0.43%	5.47%	6,593	0.97%	6.95%	10,587	1.56%
1000	NA	2.54%	3,234	0.10%	4.22%	8,664	0.28%	6.44%	16,717	0.53%
Total/Average		**100.00%**	**206**	**0.45%**	**100.00%**	**331**	**0.72%**	**100.00%**	**418**	**0.91%**

Source: CRS calculations.

Table 7. Illustrative Distributional Effects of the Proposal Under Assumed Thresholds in a Steady State With Capital Gains

Assumed threshold		$5,000			$15,000			$35,000		
AGI range ($000s)		Share of liability reduction	Average reduction per return, $	Reduction as a share of AGI	Share of liability reduction	Average reduction per return, $	Reduction as a share of AGI	Share of liability reduction	Average reduction per return, $	Reduction as a share of AGI
0	10	1.59%	18	0.63%	0.98%	20	0.68%	0.71%	20	0.68%
10	20	4.60%	60	0.40%	3.37%	77	0.52%	2.49%	78	0.52%
20	30	5.68%	97	0.39%	4.52%	136	0.55%	3.47%	143	0.58%
30	40	6.12%	146	0.42%	5.10%	214	0.61%	4.13%	237	0.68%
40	50	6.58%	208	0.46%	5.97%	330	0.74%	5.14%	389	0.87%
50	75	16.99%	317	0.52%	15.39%	504	0.82%	13.52%	606	0.99%
75	100	15.45%	622	0.72%	14.58%	1,029	1.20%	13.28%	1,283	1.49%
100	200	24.27%	1,079	0.82%	25.46%	1,982	1.50%	26.01%	2,775	2.11%
200	500	13.08%	2,188	0.76%	16.16%	4,736	1.64%	19.26%	7,730	2.67%
500	1000	3.46%	3,111	0.46%	4.97%	7,834	1.16%	6.66%	14,386	2.13%
1000	NA	2.17%	3,327	0.11%	3.49%	9,360	0.30%	5.31%	19,544	0.62%
Total/Average		**100.00%**	**247**	**0.54%**	**100.00%**	**433**	**0.94%**	**100.00%**	**593**	**1.29%**

Source: CRS calculations.

Distributional Effects

Tax proposals vary in the extent to which they benefit high income versus low income individuals. Savings subsidies typically benefit higher income individuals, who are far more likely to have significant savings. The benefits of IRAs are somewhat constrained for high income individuals compared to other savings subsidies, however, because of the dollar ceilings and, in the case of current IRAs, the income limits, which are particularly severe for traditional individual retirement accounts. This proposal raises the contribution limits and ends the income limits.

To examine the distributional effects, we return to the assumptions used to assess the general magnitude of the long run revenue estimates. **Tables 6 and 7** show for every assumed threshold what share of the total tax savings is attributable to every income class, average tax savings per return, and share of these savings in adjusted gross income (AGI) of the income class. In **Table 6**, for example, in the case of a $15,000 cap, taxpayers with AGI between $50,000 and $75,000 would receive 15.77% of the total tax savings received by all filers in all income classes. On average, each return in the group would see $394 in tax savings, which represents 0.65% of AGI.

Table 8. Number of Returns by Income Class

AGI Range ($000s)		Returns	
		Number	Share
0	10	27,456,833	21.6%
10	20	24,076,129	18.9%
20	30	18,335,165	14.4%
30	40	13,137,813	10.3%
40	50	9,955,658	7.8%
50	75	16,817,353	13.2%
75	100	7,798,113	6.1%
100	200	7,066,359	5.6%
200	500	1877722	1.5%
500	1,000	349,122	0.3%
1,000	NA	204,920	0.2%
Total		**127,075,187**	**100.0%**

Source: CRS calculations.

Current IRA provisions are designed to limit the benefits to high income individuals both through ceilings and income limits. However, a significant benefit accrues to the highest income taxpayers for this proposal. Comparing **Table 6** with **Table 8**, which contains a distribution of the population, we see, for example, that in the case of the $15,000/$30,000 assumed cap, the bottom 40% of the population gets 4% of the tax cut, the top 15 % gets about 60%, and the top 2% gets a quarter. The dollar benefit per return rises rapidly across the income classes because higher income individuals save much more that lower income ones, and, to a lesser extent, because of higher marginal tax rates.

When examining absolute tax savings or the distribution of tax benefits, high income individuals tend to have larger benefits (absent restrictions on availability through caps or exclusions) because they have much higher incomes. Almost any general tax cut would exhibit some degree of this pattern. There is a case for using, instead, a relative measure of redistribution. A way to measure the relative distribution is to examine the tax savings as a percent of income (ideally as a percent of after-tax income). This relative distribution measure still indicates a shift in relative income from lower incomes to higher incomes through most of the income distribution. Where the peak is reached depends on the cap used and the inclusion of full capital gains; however, in both **Table 6 and Table** 7, the peak generally is reached in either the $100,000 to $200,000 income class or the $200,000 to $500,000 class, suggesting that the relative benefit rises through 90% to 95% of the income distribution. Thus, except for the very wealthiest income classes (that is, the top 5% or 10% of the population), the provision increases the relative share of disposable income for higher income people — that is, redistributes income shares to the well-off

Effects on Other Types of Tax Favored Savings

The final economic consequence of a new savings account proposal, particularly one with no strings attached, is that it would reduce participation in alternative tax favored savings, as a new substitute becomes available. There are several types of tax favored uses that might be reduced, including employer pensions, standard individual retirement accounts, insurance plans, tax favored education savings accounts, tax exempt bonds, owner occupied housing, and tax favored capital gains and dividends. The displacement of tax favored accounts may be a desirable or an undesirable outcome for purposes of efficiency gains. For example, the current tax rules favor investment in owner-occupied housing, and diverting funds out of housing and into other types of investments may be desirable. The shift into passive forms of investment also favors debt finance, disfavors equity investments in unincorporated businesses, and has mixed effects on corporate equity. Encouraging employer pensions through tax benefits has some potential benefits but may also involve some distortions.

Following the release of the FY2004 proposals, much attention was focused on the effect of employer plans in discussion, and most attention will be devoted to that issue. This possible effect is cited as one of the reasons for scaling down the limits from $7,500 to $5,000.

Employer Pension Plans

Actually, the Administration proposal also proposes to simplify employer plans, including substituting Employee Retirement Savings Accounts for existing employer plans such as 401(k)s and allowing after tax (back-loaded style) employee contributions. The objective is to simplify these plans for employers (although the switch to back-loaded plans could reduce private savings and affect revenue patterns just as in the case of LSAs and RSAs).

While it is possible that the simplifications in the proposal could increase employer coverage, much more attention has been devoted to the possible effects of the individual plans on employer pension plans, particularly in the case of LSAs. Since LSAs have no strings attached, individuals might find it more attractive to reduce their voluntary 401(k) or similar contributions not matched by employer contributions and put such money instead into LSAs. Because these plans could be easily tapped for non-retirement uses, the LSAs could actually reduce retirement savings.

An even more serious issue arises with small business plans, and relates not only to the LSAs but also to the linking of benefits of highly paid employees and rank-and-file employees. Many small-business owners find setting up a plan complicated, but may still do it to make their own retirement plans (and plans of their highly compensated workers) more tax-favored. Qualification for tax purposes requires a plan to cover rank and file employees as well as owners and top officers. The basic argument made in many of these discussions is that small-business owners, finding individual retirement plans with high ceilings and, in the case of LSAs, no strings attached, will now prefer to save through individual accounts rather than by setting up retirement plans within their firms for themselves and their employees. With a $7,500 ceiling in each account (LSA and RSA), a married couple could save $30,000 per year (and save additional amounts in children's accounts).

These views have been expressed by a number of different groups and organizations. For example, the executive director of the American Society of

Pension Actuaries (ASPA) stated: "It is an understatement to suggest that the impact of these proposals on small business retirement plan coverage will be anything less than devastating."[23] Similarly, the president of the Profit-Sharing 401k Council of America (PSCA) stated: "The proposed changes significantly erode the tax code incentives that encourage employers to accept the fiduciary obligation and expense that come with offering a retirement plan ... The current approach links the availability of tax benefits for decision makers and better off workers with the retirement savings of lower paid employees. This linkage requires that employers incentivize lower paid workers to save for retirement by using expensive matching contributions as well as conducting aggressive educational campaigns."[24] Jack VanDerhei, a business professor associated with the Employee Benefit Research Institute, when commenting on the benefits of LSAs and RSAs, stated, "That's probably enough for most small employers, who could jettison doing anything for their employees and still get enough of a tax break."[25] Many other groups have made similar arguments.[26] There are also arguments that even larger employers might abandon plans because of the availability of individual tax deferred savings for their employees.

While there is no way to know for certain the effects of the proposal on employer plans, it does seem possible — and, according to the groups quoted above, likely — that the individual savings accounts, despite simplification for employer plans, ultimately reduce the coverage of employer pensions.

Individual Retirement Accounts and Life Insurance Products

Individual retirement accounts for individuals not at the limit of their combined savings could be displaced by the LSAs, which have no penalties for early withdrawal or other strings attached. Under the latest Administration proposal such conversion becomes mandatory.

Any life insurance product that has a savings elements involves a tax subsidy in the form of deferred taxes on earnings. Even term life policies if they have level premiums involve an accumulation of earnings tax free, and whole life policies explicitly provide inside buildup. Finally, life insurance companies offer plans that are particularly aimed at achieving tax benefits in the form of annuities.

Since the tax exemption benefit for LSAs and RSAs is greater than the deferral benefit, the attractiveness of these products, particularly in cases where tax reduction is a principal objective, could fall substantially.

These shifts may not involve efficiency costs — and may involve gains — but they would be disruptive for the life insurance industry.

Education Savings Accounts

Tax benefits are provided for a variety of educational savings accounts, whose tax-favored benefits depend on using the funds for educational purposes. Under the Administration's FY2007 proposals, LSAs would either displace these accounts or include them as a kind of sub-account. Although certain types of education plans could be retained, for example due to state-provided tax benefits, the attractiveness of a no-strings-attached LSA should lead to the displacement of many of the educational accounts for those who are not saving at the limit. Qualified tuition plans are more likely to remain concentrated among high income individuals, where the incentive probably matters least, and less likely to apply to moderate income individuals where the relative benefits may actually influence decisions on how much to spend on education.

Tax Exempt Bonds

Tax exempt bonds carry lower interest rates than equivalent taxable bonds. With favorable tax treatment for many other investments, the demand for tax exempt bonds should contract which would raise financing costs for state and local governments. Many analysts have criticized the tax subsidy for state and local bond finance, which is largely an accident of history and of constitutional interpretation, and might support this displacement. But it will place an additional burden on the States and localities.

Owner Occupied Housing, Debt and Business Equity

The tax exemption would shift investment into passive forms and out of equity investments in owner occupied housing and unincorporated business including rental housing). In general, the shift out of owner-occupied housing should increase economic efficiency because this type of investment is favored. The shift out of unincorporated business equity may decrease efficiency. The effects on corporate equity, the most heavily taxed type of investment, is uncertain: while the changes favor corporate equity relative to investments in other types of equity, the savings proposals also favor interest more than dividends and capital gains (which are subject to lower rates) — and thus shifts assets into debt.

SIMPLIFICATION

The Administration justifies its proposal on the grounds of simplification as well as incentives to save. For most taxpayers, the current choice is either a back-loaded or a front-loaded retirement, education, health, or other account, with restrictions more limited on back-loaded plans and income limits differing. (Individuals whose incomes exceed the ceilings can invest in a non-deductible tax-deferred account.) The proposal would replace these choices with two plans that individuals could invest in simultaneously, the RSA and the LSA. The proposal may simplify rules by eliminating disparities among currently existing tax-preferred accounts. It is important to keep in mind, though, that the substantial long-run costs of the proposal may make this simplification effort a very costly one.

Although simplification may serve as an impetus for this change, it is unclear how much simpler the resulting system would be. There would still remain a disparity between RSAs and LSAs. The LSA rules are less restrictive than those of RSA because they do not have age-based withdrawal penalties.

Furthermore, some disparities do not disappear under the FY2007 proposal but rather become less conspicuous. For example, it retains some qualified tuition plans as sub-accounts within LSAs. The funds within RSAs may be treated differently depending on their origin: rollovers from some existing accounts may be subject to various additional requirements compared to the new contributions. The FY2007 proposal would also retain limited traditional IRAs. Finally, at this point the Administration's proposal is just a conceptual framework, free of all the intricate details that ultimately determine the complexity or simplicity of the whole system.

If simplification were the principal goal, it would be much easier to permit a certain dollar amount of passive income to be excluded, without requiring the complications of keeping accounts, at least for LSAs. This approach would, however, cost more in the short run because the growth of the accounts limits the initial revenue cost.

APPENDIX A

This appendix presents the method of estimating the growth pattern of a back-loaded tax favored savings account for projecting revenue,[27] and also for determining the interest amounts in **Table 1**.

To estimate the pattern, we assumed that each year money is put into an account where it grows for 15 years and then is withdrawn as a level annuity for the next 10 years. We assumed that contributions in each case are a constant share of output. While variations in holding periods and withdrawal patterns will affect the results, this example illustrates the general pattern.

Because of the time path of a Roth IRA, the cost is very small in the beginning but grows rapidly.[28] For example, in the first year, earnings from a Roth IRA that are exempt from tax per dollar of contributions is r, where r is the interest rate, assuming an annual interest payment. In the second year, the value is $r(1+r)+r$, or slightly more than double (the first term is interest on the original first year contribution, while the second is the interest on the second year contribution).

Based on calculations assuming a 7% interest rate and a 3% growth rate (g), and keeping all measures constant relative to GDP, in the first year assets in the accounts (and revenue costs) are 3% the size of their steady-state value. By the fifth year, they are 18% of the value of the steady state size relative to GDP (which is reached in 25 years). By the 10th year, they are 41% of the size. On average, over the five-year period, the cost is 11% of the steady state cost; over a 10-year period, the cost is only one-fifth of the steady-state value relative to GDP.

A Roth-type IRA's costs are directly related to the interest rate, since they involve forgoing tax on interest. If interest rates are relatively low during the estimating period, as there is some reason to believe to be the case, the revenue loss will be even further below the steady-state values. This effect does not occur with traditional deductible IRAs, whose costs in the short run are related only to contribution levels.

Mathematically, to perform the calculations, designate the period the IRA grows prior to withdrawal as T' and the entire period the IRA exists as T. To measure the revenue cost for the Roth IRA, we estimate the cumulated value of assets in the fund. For t years in the future, t less than T', for each value of a dollar invested currently, there are e^{-gt} dollars invested that have grown at rate r, so the value of that vintage of accounts is $e^{(r-g)t}$. Integrating the value of assets yields a value at time t of:

(1) Cumulative value at time:

$$t=(e^{(r-g)t}-1)/(r-g)$$

For t greater than T' but less than T, one must take account of the value of funds that have been partially withdrawn. An annuity for a dollar that grows at rate r for T' years and then is withdrawn over (T - T') years is $e^{(rT')} r/(1-e^{-r(T-T')})$. The remaining value in the asset account is:

(2) $$V(t)=\left(\frac{e^{rT'}\left(1-e^{-r(T-t)}\right)}{1-e^{-r(T-T')}}\right)$$

when t reaches T, the numerator becomes zero.

To cumulate these amounts over time, recognize that the value in (2) is multiplied by e^{-gt}, and integrate from T' to t, to obtain:

(3) Cumulative value of (2) at time t =

$$[e^{rT'}/(1-e^{-r(T-t')})]\{e^{-gT'}-e^{-gt}/g-e^{-rT}(e^{(r-g)t}-e^{(r-g)T'})/(r-g)\}$$

For period t, t greater thanT' but less than T, the total asset value is (1) plus (3), with t set at T'in (1). For t greater than T, substitute T for t in (3) and obtain the steady state (relative to GDP) results by adding (1) and (3). If we set the second first term in the curly brackets (the one divided by r-g) to zero and multiply the result by the interest rate, the formula gives us the cumulative value of withdrawals at time t, which are relevant to traditional IRA revenue losses.

For present value calculation each year's revenue loss is discounted at rate r-g. For a constant relative to GDP cost, the share of the cost allocable to the first t years is $1-e^{-(r-g)t}$

To determine the ceilings in **Table 1**, assuming that contributions are indexed to inflation levels, note that a contribution made t years ago grows by the nominal interest r and thus has grown to a value that is e^{rt} times the original contribution. At the same time; each contribution t years ago is $e^{-\pi t}$ for each dollar today, where B is the inflation rate. Integrating over all the investments, we obtain:

(4) $$\text{Cumulative value at time } t = (e^{(r-p)^t} - 1) / (r - p)$$

and the current earnings are:

(5) $$\text{Current earnings at time } t = r(e^{(r-p)^t} - 1) / (r - p)$$

Earnings are therefore a function of the nominal interest rate, the inflation rate, and the period of time the asset has been accumulating.

End Notes

[1] There are other specialized tax-favored forms, such as medical savings accounts and educational savings accounts; the proposal allows a rollover of education accounts into LSAs. The President's proposal also includes a tax credit to sponsors of savings plans for lower income individuals, a much smaller and temporary provision, which is not considered in this analysis. The analysis also does not address proposals for simplifying and coordinating employer pension plans.

[2] The two approaches differ in several other ways. For a more complete discussion see CRS Report RL30255, *Individual Retirement Accounts (IRAs): Issues and Proposed Expansion,* by Thomas L. Hungerford and Jane G. Gravelle.

[3] The Economic Growth and Recovery Act of 2001 increased the IRA limit to $3,000 in 2002-2004, $4,000 from 2005-2007, and $5,000 in 2008 (with indexation for inflation thereafter; the provisions sunset after 2010.

[4] Beginning with FY2003, the proposal had an annual gain in revenue in the first four years: $1.4 billion, $10.6 billion, $4.8 billion, $1.9 billion. Revenue losses then occurred through FY2013: $0.6 billion, $1.8 billion, $1.9 billion, $2.45 billion, $2.7 billion, $2.9 billion, and $2.9 billion, according to the Treasury Department, *General Explanation of the Administration's 2004 Revenue Proposals*, Feb. 2003.

[5] See Joint Committee on Taxation, *Estimated Budget Effects of the Revenue Provisions Contained in the President's Fiscal Year 2004 Budget Proposal, Fiscal Years 2003-2013,* JCX-15-03, March 4, 2003. The estimate showed revenue gains from FY2003-FY2007 of $1.7 billion, $3.2 billion, $3.1 billion, $2.8 billion, and $1.4 billion. Losses occurred from FY2008-FY2013 in the amount of $0.2 billion, $1.6 billion, $2.6 billion, $3.5 billion, $4.4 billion, and $4.9 billion.

[6] Department of the Treasury, *General Explanations of the Administration's Fiscal Year 2007 Revenue Proposals,* Feb. 2006, pp. 10; Joint Committee on Taxation, *Estimated Budget Effects of the Revenue Provisions Contained in the President's Fiscal Year 2007 Budget Proposal, Fiscal Years 2006-2016* in *Description Of Revenue Provisions Contained In The President's Fiscal Year 2007 Budget Proposal*, JCS-1-06, March 2006, p. 314.

[7] Department of the Treasury, *General Explanations of the Administration's Fiscal Year 2006 Revenue Proposals,* Feb. 2005, pp. 10, 159; Department of the Treasury, *General Explanation of the Administration's 2005 Revenue Proposals*, Feb. 2004, pp. 12, 191.

[8] Joint Committee on Taxation, *Estimated Budget Effects of the Revenue Provisions Contained in the President's Fiscal Year 2005 Budget Proposal, Fiscal Years 2004-2014,* JCX-14-04 R, March 3, 2004, p. 1; Joint Committee on Taxation, *Estimated Budget Effects of the Revenue Provisions*

Contained in the President's Fiscal Year 2006 Budget Proposal, Fiscal Years 2005-2015, JCX-10-05, March 9, 2005, p. 1.

[9] For example, beginning with FY2005, the proposal had an annual gain in revenue in the first five years: $3.9 billion, $8.2 billion, $5.5 billion, $2.8 billion and $0.7 billion (there were no effects in FY2004). Revenue losses then occurred through FY2014: $0.7 billion, $2.1 billion, $3.8 billion, $4.3 billion, and $4.7 billion, according to the Treasury Department.

[10] In the short run, this offsetting gain would include the tax benefit of traditional IRA contributions, which were about $7 billion in 2000; at a 20% tax rate, worth $1.4 billion. Over 10 years, therefore, the current limits would be at least $14 billion even without accounting for growth, and would probably be considerably larger because of the rapid growth of the income limits. While the dollar limit of contributions is fixed at $2,000, temporary provisions in the 2001 tax cut allow increases in the dollar amounts to be contributed to IRAs, and the income limit will increase substantially over the period. The temporary provisions have been estimated to increase revenues by about $25 billion over 10 years. If we use the conservative $14 billion number and add the $25 billion, there are temporary 10-year gains of $39 billion embedded in the estimates and without those temporary gains, the gain of $2 billion for the $7,500 limit would be a loss of $37 billion. Based on the projections discussed above, the long-run steady-state cost would be five times as large or $185 billion, leading to an annual loss of about $18.5 billion. With the higher revenues reported for the FY2005 estimates (with the lower ceiling) the $39 billion would be offset by about $6 billion, for a loss of $33 billion — suggesting a total of $177 billion over 10 years, or an annual about $17 billion. Note that this analysis assumes that additional accounts would be diverted from existing accounts, and not associated with additional private savings. See the section on savings effects for a justification of this assumption.

[11] For the FY2004 Administration estimates, the appropriate year would be 2008, where the revenue cost is estimated at $1.8 billion. However, this $1.8 billion is the net of a positive gain from substitutions for front-loaded IRAs and the loss from additional back-loaded IRAs. The cost for the 2001 increases for that year was projected at $3.4 billion, and if we use a $1.4 billion cost for current IRAs, the results imply a loss of $6.6 billion — which would translate into an annual loss of $37 billion ($6.6 billion divided by 0.18) per year ($370 billion over 10 years). This estimate fixes the existing loss of front loaded IRAs at only $1.4 billion; if it were raised to $2 billion, the cost would $40 billion (($2+$3.4+$1.8)X0.1/0.18. Applying the same methods to the new 2005 estimates with the lower limit results but using 2010 (the 2005 proposal is made a year later and delays the effective date by another year), the proposal loses $0.7 billion. However, the gain from the temporary limit increase is $4.4 billion, implying a loss after backing out the temporary revenue gain of $6.5 billion, which would lead to a cost of $36 billion, also close to $40 billion if the value of current IRAs was increased.

[12] In the steady state the loss from back-loaded accounts is the interest rate times the asset balance. The loss for a front-loaded account includes this forgone interest but it is reduced by the gain from tax on withdrawals less the loss from the tax benefit of the deductions. See Jane G. Gravelle, "Estimating the Long-Run Revenue Effects of Tax Law Changes," *Eastern Economics Journal*, vol. 19, fall 1993, pp. 481-494.

[13] Internal Revenue Service, Statistics of Income Division, Individual Statistics Branch, *1999 Public Use Tax File*, Jan. 28, 2003. The data in this file are blurred (actual returns are averaged and some other changes are made) in order to protect taxpayer confidentiality. These data are the most recent available. We also use the tax rates in force in 1999, which are different from the current rates, but consistent with permanent rates.

[14] See Jane G. Gravelle, *The Economic Effects of Taxing Capital Income,* Cambridge, MIT Press, 1994, p. 130; Leonard E. Burman, *The Labyrinth of Capital Gains Tax Policy*, Washington, D.C., The Brookings Institution, 1999, p.25; Janette Wilson, "Sales of Capital Assets Reported on Individual Income Tax Returns, 1999, Internal Revenue Service, *Statistics of Income Bulletin*, summer 2003, pp. 132-154.

[15] Leonard E. Burman, William G. Gale, and Peter Orszag, "The Administration's Savings Proposals: Preliminary Analysis," *Tax Notes*, March 3, 2003, pp. 1423-1446.

[16] Joint Committee on Taxation, "Estimates of Federal Tax Expenditures for Fiscal Years 2004-2008," December 22, 2003.

[17] A recent CBO working paper, "A Steady-state Analysis of Proposals to Reduce the Tax on Saving," by Paul Burnham, February 2006, estimated a loss of $17 billion per year in a steady state, well above the official annual cost estimates of the first ten years of the program. The estimate appears to reflect an assumption that only 20% of corporate stocks can be shifted into these accounts. The author gives no rationale behind this assumption, and due to a very non-restrictive nature of the proposed accounts, it may be conservative.

[18] For a more complete discussion of the savings literature, see Jane G. Gravelle, *The Economic Effects of Taxing Capital Income* (Cambridge, MA., MIT Press, 1994), p. 27 for a discussion of the general empirical literature on savings and pp. 193-197 for a discussion of the empirical studies of IRAs. Subsequent to this survey, a paper by Orazio P. Attanasio and Thomas C. DeLeire, "The Effect of Individual Retirement Accounts on Household Consumption and National Savings," *Economic Journal*, vol.112, July 2002, pp. 504-538, was published. That study found little evidence that IRAs increased savings. For additional surveys see the three articles published in the fall 1996 *Journal of Economic Perspectives,* vol. 10: R. Glenn Hubbard and Jonathan Skinner, "Assessing the Effectiveness of Savings Incentives," (pp. 73-90); James M. Poterba, Steven F. Venti and David A. Wise, "How Retirement Savings Programs Increase Saving," (pp. 91-113); Eric M. Engen, William G. Gale, and John Karl Scholz, "The Illusory Effects of Savings Incentives on Saving," (pp. 113-138). An International Monetary Fund working paper by Alun Thomas and Christopher Towe, "U.S. Private Saving and the Tax Treatment of IRA/401(k)s: A Re-examination Using Household Saving Data," Aug. 1996, found that IRAs did not increase private household saving. A study by Eric M. Engen, Federal Reserve Board, and William G. Gale, Brookings Institution, found that 401(k) plans, which are similar to IRAs in some ways, did not have much effect on savings. See "Debt, Taxes, and the Effects of 401(k) Plans on Household Wealth Accumulation," May 1997. A recent simulation study in the *American Economic Review*, while not based on direct empirical evidence, suggests only a small fraction of IRA contributions represent net savings. See Ayse Imrohoroglu, Selahattin Imrohoroglu, and Douglas H. Joines, "The Effect of Tax-Favored Accounts on Capital Accumulation," vol. 88, Sept. 1998, pp. 749-768.

[19] This material has been presented by Steve Venti and David Wise in several papers; see, for example, "Have IRAs Increased U.S. Savings?," *Quarterly Journal of Economics*, vol. 105, Aug. 1990, pp. 661-698.

[20] See William G. Gale and John Karl Scholz, "IRAs and Household Savings," *American Economic Review*, Dec. 1994, pp. 1233-1260. A detailed explanation of the modeling problem with the Venti and Wise study is presented in Jane G. Gravelle, "Do Individual Retirement Accounts Increase Savings?," *Journal of Economic Perspectives*, vol. 5, spring 1991, pp. 133-148.

[21] See Douglas H. Joines and James G. Manegold, "IRAs and Savings: Evidence from a Panel of Taxpayers," University of Southern California; Orazio P. Attanasio and Thomas C. DeLeire, "IRA's and Household Saving Revisited: Some New Evidence," National Bureau of Economic Research Working Paper 4900, October 1994.

[22] See CRS Report RS20224, *The Collapse of Household Savings: Why Has It Happened and What Are Its Implications?*, By Brian Cashell and Gail Makinen.

[23] "ASPA Opposes Bush Administration Savings Initiative," ASPA Press Release, February 2, 2003.

[24] "President's Proposals Will Reduce the Appeal of Employer Plans," PSCA Press Release, February 5, 2003.

[25] This statement is quoted in Aaron Bernstein, "Bush's Retirement Rx is Bad Medicine," *Business Week Online*, February 18, 2003, [http://www.businessweek.com/careers/content/feb2003/ca20030218_8886_ca030.htm], visited December 31, 2003.

[26] Criticisms have also been made by the American Institute of Certified Public Accountants (AICPA) Tax Section (whose letter was the subject of a September 2, 2003 response from the Treasury Department). See also the comments reported in CRS Report RS21541, *Retirement Savings Accounts: The President's Budget Proposal for 2004*, by Patrick Purcell.

[27] The pattern of both forms is estimated in Jane G. Gravelle, "Estimating Long run Revenue Effects of Tax Law Changes," *Eastern Economic Journal*, vol. 19, Fall 1993, pp. 481-494.

[28] This revenue cost assumes that Roth IRAs displace other investments, a finding consistent with empirical evidence and with economic theory (which suggest that these provisions can either decrease or increase savings). In any case, the *relative* pattern of costs should be similar as long as some cost occurs.

CHAPTER SOURCES

The following chapters have been previously published:

Chapter 1 – This is an edited, excerpted and augmented edition of a United States Congressional Research Service publication,

Report Order Code RL30708, dated January 17, 2008.

Chapter 2 – This is an edited, excerpted and augmented edition of a United States Congressional Research Service publication.

Report Order Code RL33112, dated October 15, 2007.

Chapter 3 – This is an edited, excerpted and augmented edition of a United States Congressional Research Service publication.

Report Order Code RL33168, dated January 9, 2008.

Chapter 4 - This is an edited, excerpted and augmented edition of a United States Congressional Research Service publication.

Report Order Code RL33482, dated September 27, 2007.

Chapter 5 - This is an edited, excerpted and augmented edition of a United States Congressional Research Service publication.

Report Order Code RS21480, updated July 31, 2008.

Chapter 6 - This is an edited, excerpted and augmented edition of a United States Congressional Research Service publication.

Report Order Code RL32228, updated March 7, 2007.

INDEX

D

E

H

I

J

K

L

R

S

T

U